C I T Y P A C K
Prague

By Michael Ivory

3RD EDITION

Fodor's Travel Publications
New York • Toronto • London • Sydney • Auckland

WWW.FODORS.COM

Contents

life 5–12

how to organize your time 13–22

top 25 sights 23–48

About this book

Citypack Prague is divided into six sections to cover the six most important aspects of your visit to Prague:

- The city and its people
- Itineraries, walks, and excursions
- The top 25 sights to visit
- Features about different aspects of the city that make it special
- Restaurants, hotels, stores, and nightlife
- Practical information

In addition, easy to read side panels provide extra facts and snippets, highlights of places to visit, and invaluable practical advice.

CROSS-REFERENCES

To help you make the most of your visit, cross-references, indicated by ➤, show you where to find additional information about a place or subject.

MAPS

The fold-out map in the wallet at the back of the book is a comprehensive street plan of Prague. All the map references given in the book refer to this map. For example, the Národní divadlo (National Theater) on Národní 2, Nové město, has the following information: ➕ D/E5—indicating the grid squares of the map in which the National Theater will be found.

The downtown maps found on the inside front and back covers of the book itself are for quick reference. They show the top 25 sights, described on pages 24–48, which are clearly plotted by number (❶ – ㉕, not page number) from west to east.

ADMISSION CHARGES

An indication of the admission charge (for all attractions) is given by categorizing the standard adult rate as follows:
✋ expensive (over Kč200), moderate (Kč50–Kč200), inexpensive (Kč50 or less).

PRAGUE *life*

INTRODUCING PRAGUE

St. Nicholas's Church, seen from Hradčany

"Golden Prague," "Prague the hundred-towered," "the most beautiful city in Europe": such clichés are certainly true, though they tell only part of the story. Ocher in color, many of the city's buildings can gleam like gold, especially in the glow of the late afternoon sun; the skyline is punctuated by the uncountable towers, turrets, and steeples; and Prague's beauty is incontestable.

The site is superb, with rock bluffs above a broad and curving river, and steep slopes rising through orchards and woodland. Human activities have enhanced what nature provided so generously, crowning the heights with great churches and palaces, emphasizing the slopes with terraced gardens, precipitous streets, and flights of stairs, and marking the course of the river with a sequence of foaming weirs and bold bridges.

Over a thousand years of history is expressed in stone: the foundations of the first Christian churches can still be seen, while below the sidewalks of the Old Town are vaulted cellars that once formed the first floor of medieval merchants' houses. In the 17th and 18th centuries the baroque style transformed the city's appearance. In the 19th century came great landmarks such as the National Museum and National Theater—testimony to the Czech nation's self-confidence—followed by the extravagances of art nouveau. Even the radical architects of the first half of the 20th century managed to insert their innovative buildings into the urban scene with a minimum of disturbance.

Urban decay

Visitors are sometimes shocked at the shabby state of some of Prague's buildings. Under Communism, showpieces were restored at great public expense, but less favored buildings moldered away, encased in straitjackets of scaffolding to stop them from falling into the street. Privatization and restitution, the return of property to its former owners, has gone far to remedy the situation.

6

In spite of—or perhaps as a result of—military defeats, occupation, and denial of citizens' rights, the four distinct quarters that form Prague's historic core are in a near-perfect state of preservation. They are the Castle district (Hradčany), the Lesser Town (Malá Strana) at its foot, the Old Town (Staré město) across the river, and the New Town (Nové město) laid out in the 14th century.

Beyond is a ring of rundown suburbs, largely 19th-century, then an outer circle of high-rise housing projects and satellite towns built during the last 40 years. These suburbs are where most Praguers live. For many, life after Communism remains gray, the struggle to make ends meet greater than ever. Others have embraced the new freedom with alacrity; there's enjoyment in the previously forbidden pleasures of making and spending money. The stream of visitors from abroad adds an extra element of vibrancy and has vastly improved the quality of dining and lodging options. Entrepreneurs are everywhere, opening stores, cafés, and bars. There's excitement in the air, particularly among the young, as Prague claims its rightful place in a Europe from which it has been long excluded.

Get lost

Prague is a labyrinth, a warren of winding roads and alleyways, courtyards and passageways leading deep into buildings. Don't worry about getting lost—treat disorientation as a pleasure and enjoy the unexpected treats along the way. The historic center is small, and sooner or later you will recognize a landmark or emerge by the riverside.

Míšeňská Street, Malá Strana

PRAGUE IN FIGURES

Geography
- Capital of the Czech Republic (and until 1993 of Czechoslovakia), Prague is located in Central Europe, on the River Vltava.
- 50° 5' north and 14° 25' east.
- Area: 191sq miles.
- Lowest point (River Vltava): 577 feet above sea level.
- Highest point (Kopanina): 1,299 feet above sea level.
- Distance from Berlin: 217 miles.
- Distance from Vienna: 181 miles.
- Distance from Paris: 643 miles.
- Distance from London: 853 miles.

People
- Population: 1,225,000; 95.5 percent Czech.
- Living conditions: About half the population lives in *paneláks*, high-rise apartments built under Communism. The largest housing project is Southwest Town, with a population planned to reach 140,000.
- Weekends: Half of Prague's population leaves the city on summer weekends, many to spend time in their *chata*, or country cottage.
- Students: 43,000 attend city universities.
- Food and Drink: The Czech Republic is known for its beer and Czechs drink an average of 160 liters per person per year. They are also big meat eaters.

Environment
- Conservation: The city's historic core, designated by UNESCO as being of world importance, covers an area of 2,224 acres and includes some 10,000 protected artifacts and works of art.
- Green space: The city has nearly 25,000 acres of parks, cemeteries, etc.
- Vehicles: Nearly 750,000 fill 1,738 miles of streets.
- Metro: 27 miles long, with 46 stations, it carries more than a third of all the city's public transportation passengers. There are more than 80 miles of tram lines within the city.
- Pollution: In Prague it's heavy. Industries, heating plants, and motor vehicles emit more than 30,000 tons of sulfur dioxide per year.

CONTEMPORARY PRAGUE PEOPLE

VÁCLAV HAVEL

Playwright and one-time prominent dissident President Havel, by attempting to combine political activity with ethical principles, has not always endeared himself to market-obsessed politicians keen to rush the new republic into the embrace of modern capitalism. Gruff of voice and short of stature, Havel has survived ill-treatment by secret police and a chain-smoking past, but his shaky state of health is a cause for concern for many citizens, who see him as an irreplaceable asset to this fledgling democracy.

IVAN PLICKA

Plicka has spent most of his working life as an engineer in the section of the City Architect's Department responsible for the planning of Greater Prague. Now near retirement, he is proud of the city's beauty and of his office's role in preserving it. He hopes

Engineer Ivan Plicka

that his department's masterplan for Prague in the new millennium will protect the downtown from the commercial pressures that have destroyed the traditional character of many western cities.

LENKA CHOBOTOVÁ

Lenka, one of a generation of young people who experienced Communism only as a small child, graduated from a high school specializing in information sciences. A six-month stay in Britain gave her fluency in English, and she hopes to study English literature at one of Prague's universities, though for the time being she is happy to earn a modest living as a librarian. Cheerful and outgoing, Lenka has a zest for life that expresses itself in getting together with like-minded friends to sing and make music in one of the city's pubs.

Jo Williams

Art historian Jo hails from New York City and is one of a number of young Americans attracted to post-Communist Prague. An enthusiast for Czech culture, she has not only mastered the language but works in a Czech environment at a local salary, helping to raise the profile of an arts foundation. Her first job involved promoting abroad the hidden treasures of the National Gallery's modern art collection in the Veletržní palác (➤ 47).

A Chronology

7th or 8th century AD	Prague's legendary foundation by Princess Libuše and her plowman husband, Přemysl.
Late 9th century	A Slav stronghold is established on Hradčany Hill, where Prince Bořivoj builds the first timber church.
10th century	Trading settlements are set up in Lesser Town (Malá Strana) and Old Town (Staré město).
1231	King Wenceslas I fortifies the Old Town with 13 towers, 39-foot-high walls, and a moat (today's Na příkopě, or Moat Street).
1253–78	Reign of King Otakar II, who extends and fortifies Malá Strana, inviting German merchants and traders to settle there.
1346–78	Under King/Emperor Charles IV, St. Vitus's Cathedral is begun, the New Town (Nové město) is laid out, and Charles Bridge is built.
1415	Religious reformer Jan Hus is burned at the stake for heresy.
1576–1611	Reign of eccentric Emperor Rudolph II.
1620	Battle of the White Mountain just outside Prague, in which the Protestant army is routed. In the following years, Protestant leaders are executed in Old Town Square. Czechs who refuse to reconvert to Catholicism emigrate en masse. A largely foreign nobility is installed, loyal to the Habsburgs, and Prague is beautified with Baroque churches and palaces. The court makes Vienna its principal seat, and Prague becomes a sleepy provincial town.
1848	A revolt led by students is put down by Austrian General Windischgrätz, but Czech nationalism continues to grow.
1914–18	Czechs are dragged into World War I on the Austrian side. Many soldiers desert or join the Czech Legion fighting for the Allies in Russia, Italy, and France.

1918   Establishment of the democratic First
Republic of Czechoslovakia under liberal
President Tomáš Masaryk.

1938   Britain and France agree to cede the
Sudetenland to Hitler's Germany, depriving
Czechoslovakia of most of its industry and
all its defenses.

1939   Hitler dismembers what is left of Czechoslovakia.
The Czech provinces become the "Protector-
ate of Bohemia-Moravia," and Prague is
declared the "Fourth City of the Third Reich."

1942   The assassination of Reichsprotektor Heydrich
by Czechoslovak parachutists flown in from
Britain leads to brutal repression by the Nazis.

1945   The people of Prague liberate their city and
welcome in the Red Army. Over 2.5 million
Germans are expelled from the Sudetenland.

1948   Communists, the most powerful party in the
democratically elected government, stage a
coup d'état. Stalinist repression follows.

1968   The Prague Spring, an attempt to change
Communism into "Socialism with a human
face," is crushed by Soviet tanks.

1977   Dissident intellectuals sign Charter 77, a call
for the government to apply the Helsinki
Agreements of 1975. Many, including Václav
Havel, are harassed and imprisoned on
trumped-up charges.

1989   The Velvet Revolution. The Communist
government resigns and is replaced by the
dissident-led Civic Forum. Václav Havel is
elected president.

1993   Czechoslovakia splits into the independent
states of Slovakia and the Czech Republic
(with Prague as the latter's capital).

1999   The Czech Republic joins the NATO alliance.   11

PEOPLE & EVENTS FROM HISTORY

Fall from power

Yet another Prague defenestration (not officially referred to as such) was the fall of much-loved foreign minister Jan Masaryk from his office window in the Černinský palác (Černin Palace) when the Communists seized power in 1948. His opposition to Communism led many to think that he was pushed, but it is more likely that he jumped, in despair at the prospect facing his country and at his powerlessness to prevent it.

DEFENESTRATIONS

Prague's history is marked by several defenestrations—in which political opponents were pushed from upper-floor windows. In 1419 a crowd of Hussites was pelted with stones from the New Town Hall by their German Catholic adversaries. The angry mob stormed the building and threw the culprits from the upstairs windows onto Charles Square, where they were killed. In 1483 the mayor of Prague was thrown out of a window of the Old Town Hall, and in 1618 a group of Protestant noblemen forcibly entered Prague Castle and hurled two Catholic councillors into the dung-heaps below. The victims' survival—the manure broke their fall—was attributed to divine intervention.

IMPERIAL SPLENDOR

The erudite, unstable Habsburg emperor Rudolph II transferred the imperial capital from Vienna to Prague in 1583. His interests, ranging from astronomy to erotic art, flourished in his adopted city. Never a politician, the faltering ruler was forced to delegate his powers to his brother, Matthias, who returned the Court to Vienna in 1612, the year of Rudolph's death.

Alexander Dubček

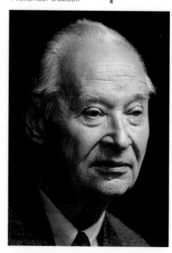

FALSE SPRING

By the mid-1960s, Communist oppression in Czechoslovakia was all too apparent. In what came to be known as the "Prague Spring" of 1968, the party, under Alexander Dubček, promised to create "Socialism with a human face." Terrified at this prospect, the Soviet Union sent in tanks in August and took the government off to Moscow in chains. A humiliated Dubček was first told to reverse his reforms, and then dismissed. Two decades of social and political winter followed, ended by the Velvet Revolution in 1989.

PRAGUE
how to organize your time

ITINERARIES

These four itineraries, all beginning from the "Golden Cross"—the pedestrianized area where Václavské náměstí (Wenceslas Square) meets Národní and Na příkopě—are based on Prague's four historic districts.

ITINERARY ONE	**OLD TOWN & JOSEFOV**
Morning	Walk east along Na příkopě (Moat Street). Obecní dům (Municipal House ➤ 46). Walk along Celetná to Staroměstské náměstí (Old Town Square ➤ 42). Coffee at one of the cafés in the square. Climb the tower of the Old Town Hall. Orloj (Astronomical Clock ➤ 59). Take in Kostel Panny Marie Před Týnem (Týn Church ➤ 55). Walk along Pařížská to the Staronová synagóga (Old/New Synagogue ➤ 39).
Lunch	Restaurant on Pařížská (Paris Boulevard).
Afternoon	Starý židovský hřbitov (Old Jewish Cemetery ➤ 40). Uměleckoprůmyslové muzeum (Decorative Arts Museum ➤ 37).
ITINERARY TWO	**HRADČANY, THE CASTLE HILL**
Morning	Go west along 28 října and Národní. Catch tram 22 or 23 at the Národní třída stop (Bílá Hora direction) to the Pohořelec stop. Strahovský klášter (Strahov Monastery ➤ 24). Coffee in Pohořelec Square. Continue to Loretánská kaple (the Loretto Shrine ➤ 26). Follow Černínská Street to Nový Svět (➤ 25). Pražský hrad (Prague Castle ➤ 29).
Lunch	One of the restaurants near the castle.
Afternoon	Katedrála sv. Víta (St. Vitus's Cathedral ➤ 30). Bazilika sv. Jiří (St. George's Basilica ➤ 31). Head through the castle gardens (➤ 58) and go via Nerudova (➤ 32) to Malostranské náměstí (Malá Strana Square). Return to the Golden Cross by tram 22 or on foot over the Karlův most (Charles Bridge).

ITINERARY THREE	OVER THE BRIDGE TO MALÁ STRANA
Morning	Enter the Old Town via Na můstku and Havelská ulička. Turn left into the market held on Havelská and V kotcích streets, and continue west via Uhelný trh and Skořepka to Betlémské náměstí (Bethlehem Square). Betlémská kaple (Bethlehem Chapel ► 55). Náprstkovo muzeum (► 53). Coffee in Betlémské náměstí. Follow Husova Street and turn left onto the Royal Way on Karlova Street. Cross Karlův most (Charles Bridge). Turn right into Josefská and again to Letenská. Valdštejnský palác (Wallenstein Palace ► 34).
Lunch	Malostranské náměstí (Malá Strana Square).
Afternoon	Chrám sv. Mikuláše (► 33). Schönborn and Lobkovic Palaces (► 54). Walk via Mostecká and Lázeňská to Maltézské náměstí (Maltese Square) and Velkopřevorské náměstí (Grand Priors' Square) with the John Lennon Wall. Cross the Čertovka brook to Na kampě on Kampa Island. Return via Most Legií (Legions' Bridge) and the Národní divadlo (National Theater ► 36).

ITINERARY FOUR	NEW TOWN & VYŠEHRAD
Morning	Walk west into Jungmannovo náměstí. Enjoy the Františkánská zahrada (Franciscans' Garden) behind Kostel Panny Marie Sněžné (Church of Our Lady of the Snows). Václavské náměstí (► 43); stop for coffee. Národní muzeum (National Museum ► 44).
Lunch	Restaurant or café in Václavské náměstí.
Afternoon	Metro to Vyšehrad. Congress Center. Go west along Na Bučance and V pevnosti. Vyšehrad (► 38). Tram 3, then back to Václavské náměstí via Vodičkova and the Novák building (► 56).

15

WALKS

THE SIGHTS

- Old Town Hall (➤ 42)
- Clam-Gallas Palace
- Old Town Bridge Tower
  (➤ 35)
- Karlův most (Charles Bridge
  ➤ 35)
- Chrám sv. Mikuláše (St.
  Nicholas's Church ➤ 33)
- Nerudova (➤ 32)

INFORMATION

Distance 1.2 miles
Time 1 hour
Start point Staroměstské náměstí
(Old Town Square)
⊞ E4
Ⓜ Staroměstská
End point Hradčanské náměstí
(Hradčany Square)
⊞ C4
🚊 Tram 22, 23

Surface
restoration

With their often ambivalent attitude
to tradition, the Communists
decided to promote the Royal Way
(see Walk) as a tourist route,
restoring the buildings along it. But
the treatment was sometimes more
of a face-lift than a complete
rejuvenation.

IN THE FOOTSTEPS OF KINGS—THE OLD TOWN TO THE CASTLE

This walk follows the Royal Way, the ancient coronation route taken by Czech kings from their downtown residence to the cathedral high up in Hradčany. It starts in Staroměstské náměstí (Old Town Square) and is popular, so you are likely to have plenty of company.

Go west into Malé náměstí (Little Square), with its delightful fountain, and turn into twisting Karlova Street, with its tempting gift shops. The street's final curve brings you into Křižovnicke náměstí (Knights of the Cross Square). Look out for the traffic as you rush to enjoy the incomparable view of the castle across the river.

Pass through the Old Town Bridge Tower onto Karlův most (Charles Bridge); admire the stunning procession of saintly statues that adorns its parapets. As it approaches Malá Strana, the bridge becomes a flyover, then, after the Malá Strana Bridge Tower, it leads you to Mostecká (Bridge) Street. Cross Malostranské náměstí (Malá Strana Square), dominated by the great bulk of Chrám sv. Mikuláše (St. Nicholas's Church), with care. Grit your teeth in preparation for the climb up Nerudova, and don't forget to turn sharp right onto the final leg of the castle approach, Ke hradu. Regain your breath while leaning on the wall of Hradčanské náměstí (Hradčany Square) and soak up the panorama of the city far below, a just reward for the climb.

Ceiling in the Schwarzenberg Palace

THE SIGHTS

- Švarcenberský palác (➤ 54)
- Strahovský klášter (Strahov Monastery ➤ 24)
- Černínský palác (➤ 54)
- Loretánská kaple (Loretto Shrine ➤ 26)
- Nový Svět (➤ 25)
- Šternberský palác (➤ 27)
- Arcibiskupský palác (➤ 54)
- Královská Zahrada (Royal Gardens ➤ 58)
- Letenské sady (Letná Plain ➤ 50)
- Josefov, the Ghetto (➤ 39, 40)

INFORMATION

Distance 2.5 miles
Time 2 hours
Start point Hradčanské náměstí (Hradčany Square)
🚹 C4
🚋 Tram 22, 23
End point Staroměstské náměstí (Old Town Square)
🚹 E4
🚇 Staroměstská

BACK TO THE OLD TOWN VIA SOME OF PRAGUE'S GARDENS

From Hradčanské náměstí walk up Loretánská Street, making a U-turn left as you enter Pohořelec Square. A short way down Úvoz, make a sharp right and stop to enjoy the view from the vineyard lying just below Strahovský klášter (Strahov Monastery). Go through the monastery courtyard, turning right into Pohořelec, then left into Loretánské náměstí. Černínska Street leads downhill into Nový Svět.

Return to Hradčanské náměstí via Nový Svět and Kanovnická. Go through the Matthias Gate of the castle, then out of the north gate from the castle's Second Courtyard. Turn into the Královská zahrada (Royal Gardens); leave them near the Belvedere summer palace and enter the Chotkovy sady (Chotek Gardens). Cross the footbridge into Letenské sady (Letná Plain), and view the city from the Hanavský pavilon, then from the plinth where Stalin's statue stood. Descend the steps and ramps to the Čechův most (Čech Bridge) and return to Staroměstské náměstí via Josefov—the former Jewish ghetto.

Rustic retreat

The tiny vineyard below Strahov Monastery is a leftover from the days when vines clad most of the slopes hereabouts. Young apple, pear, cherry, and almond trees have been planted.

17

EVENING STROLLS

STARÉ MĚSTO (THE OLD TOWN)

Survey the busy downtown scene from the terrace in front of the Národní muzeum (National Museum) at the top of Václavské náměstí (Wenceslas Square) before leaving through the underpass (don't try to cross the road) and walk down either side of the square. Keep going in the same direction at the foot of the square, along Na můstku and Melantrichova into Staroměstské náměstí (Old Town Square). Follow the Royal Way (► 16), turning left into Husova, then right into Betlémské náměstí (Bethlehem Square), a quieter focus of nightlife. Head down Náprstkova and join the Vltava embankment, crossing the road carefully. The best point to absorb the view of the river, Malá Strana, and the castle is from the tip of Novotného lávka, by the statue of Smetana.

INFORMATION

Staré město (The Old Town)
Distance 1 mile
Time 1 hour
Start point Národní muzeum
(National Museum)
🚊 F5
🚇 Muzeum
End point Smetana statue
(► 50)
🚊 D4
🚇 Staroměstská

View over Malá Strana and the Old Town

MALÁ STRANA

Finish your beer or coffee in one of the cafés by the Smetana statue and go through the arcade leading to Křižovnicke náměstí (Knights of the Cross Square) at the Old Town end of Karlův most (Charles Bridge). Continue in the same direction, then cross the Vltava by the Mánesův most (bridge). Head for Malostranská Metro station and walk through what is probably the only subway garden in the world to palace-lined Valdštejnská Street, with its unusual view of the castle above. Tomášská leads into Malostranské náměstí. Return to the Smetana statue down Mostecká and across Karlův most, which is particularly enchanting at night.

INFORMATION

Malá Strana
Distance 2 miles
Time 1½ hours
Start and end point
Smetana statue (► 50)
🚊 D4
🚇 Staroměstská

ORGANIZED TOURS

There are plenty of general tours of the city, as well as more detailed explorations of particular districts and trips that venture out into the surroundings. The difficulty lies in choosing among them. The best advice is to shop around and consider all the alternatives.

PRAGUE INFORMATION SERVICE

A good starting point for finding out about the organized tours available during your visit is the official Prague Information Service (Pražská informační služba—PIS) ✉ Na příkopě 20, Nové město ☎ 2422 6097 🕐 Winter: Mon–Fri 9–6; Sat 9–3. Summer: Mon–Fri 9–7; Sat–Sun 9–5 🚇 Náměstí Republiky; ✉ Staroměstské náměstí 1 (Old Town Hall) ☎ 2448 2018 🕐 Winter Mon–Fri 9–6; Sat–Sun 9–5. Summer Mon–Fri 9–7; Sat–Sun 9–6 🚇 Staroměstská or Můstek

PIS also runs its own tours in a reliable way.

MAIN TOUR OPERATORS

Čedok, the longest-established travel company in Prague, can be found at ✉ Na příkopě 18, Nové město ☎ 2419 7111; fax 2224 4421 🚇 Náměstí Republiky; ✉ Rytířská 16, Staré město ☎ 2422 5673 🚇 Můstek or Staroměstská; ✉ Ruzyně Airport ☎ 2056 0576;
Premiant City Tour ✉ Na příkopě 23, Nové město ☎ 0601 212625 (mobile)

WALKING TOURS

A main starting point for themed walks downtown is Staroměstské náměstí (Old Town Square); check local posters for starting times.
Also try Prague Walks ☎ 6121 4603 or 0601 235213

BOAT TOURS

Boat tours along the Vltava range from short, hour-long trips to long excursions that include lunch or dinner.
EVD 🏳 E3 ✉ Quayside at Na Františku (near the southern end of Čechův most) ☎ 231 0208 or 231 1915 🚇 Staroměstská
PPS 🏳 D5 ✉ Rašínovo nábřeží (south of Jiráskův most) ☎ 2493 1013 🚇 Karlovo náměstí

Castle tour

A stroll around Pražský hrad (Prague Castle) in the company of a well-informed guide can be instructive. Tours start from the castle's Information Center (🏳 C4 ✉ Hradčany ☎ 2437 3368) in the Third Courtyard, opposite the main doors of Katedrála sv. Víta (St Vitus's Cathedral).

View across the River Vltava to Prague Castle

19

EXCURSIONS

Hrad Karlštejn

INFORMATION

Hrad Karlštejn

- ✉ Hrad Karlštejn
- ☎ 7400 8154 (reservations)
  0311 68 16 17 (castle)
- 🕐 Apr, Oct: daily 9–noon, 1–4.
  May–Sep: daily 9–noon,
  1–5 (–6 Jul, Aug). Nov:
  daily 9–noon, 1–5. Winter:
  check locally
- 🚆 Suburban trains from
  Prague-Smíchov to Karlštejn:
  travel time 40 min

Zámek Mělník (Mělník Castle)

- ✉ Svatováclavská, Mělník
- ☎ 0206 62 21 21
- 🕐 Mar–Dec: daily 10–5.
  Winter: check locally
- 🚌 Bus from Nádraží Holešovice
  metro/bus/train station:
  travel time 50 minutes

*Right: A warrior at
Zámek Konopiště*

HRAD KARLŠTEJN (KARLŠTEJN CASTLE)

This mighty fortress, one of the great sights of Bohemia, towers above the glorious woodlands of the gorge of the River Berounka. The superb panorama from the castle walls will compensate you for the long climb up. The name of the castle, which was started in 1348, celebrates the Emperor Charles IV. He conceived it as a sort of sacred bunker, a repository for the Crown Jewels and his collection of holy relics. The castle was also planned as a personal, processional way that the emperor would follow to its climax—the Great Tower containing the Chapel of the Holy Rood, reached only after much prayer and contemplation. This gorgeous chamber has at last been reopened, its gilded walls lined with semi-precious stones and hung with 129 panel paintings of holy personages—a triumph of High Gothic art.

MĚLNÍK

Built on a bluff near the confluence of the Vltava and Elbe rivers, this ancient town is famous for the vineyards that rise up in terraces beneath its imposing castle. Following the demise of Communism, Mělník's castle and estates have been returned to the original aristocratic Lobkovic owners. Long before the Lobkovic family, however, it was a royal seat, the abode of the Czech queens, one of whom raised her grandson Wenceslas (later the "Good King") here. The castle courtyard, with its Gothic and Renaissance wings and ancient wine cellars, is approached via the charmingly arcaded town square.

LIDICE

Nowhere could seem more ordinary than this modern little mining village in the dull countryside just beyond Prague airport. But on June 10, 1942, on the flimsiest of pretexts, its male population was shot and its women and children

Zámek Mělník

INFORMATION

Lidice

✉ Monument: 10 června 1942

☎ 0312 25 30 63

🕓 Jan–Mar, Nov–Dec: daily 9–3. Apr–Oct: daily 8–5

🚇 From Dejvická Metro stop

Zámek Konopiště

✉ Zámek Konopiště, Benešov u Prahy

☎ 0301 72 13 66

🕓 Apr, Oct: Tue–Sun 9–noon, 1–3. May–Aug: Tue–Sun 9–noon, 1–5. Sep: Tue–Sun 9–noon, 1–4. Winter: check locally

🚉 Hlavní nádraží to Benešov (travel time 1 hour), then take bus or taxi, or follow marked path for 2 miles

sent off to a concentration camp—and Lidice's name resounded round the world as a synonym for Czech suffering and German ruthlessness. Days before, Reichsprotektor Heydrich had been assassinated, and the Nazis needed revenge. Lidice was razed to the ground and its name removed from the records "forever." After the war the village was rebuilt a short distance away, while the site of the atrocity became a memorial museum and park.

ZÁMEK KONOPIŠTĚ (KONOPIŠTĚ CASTLE)

Konopiště Castle's round towers rise in romantic fashion above the surrounding woodlands. The palace's origins go back to the 14th century, but it owes its present appearance largely to Archduke Franz Ferdinand, heir to the Habsburg throne, who acquired it in 1887. The corridors are filled with trophies of the countless wild creatures he slaughtered while waiting for the demise of his long-lived uncle Franz Joseph. The archduke met his own violent end when he was cut down by an assassin's bullet in Sarajevo, thereby triggering the start of World War I. The castle is full of Franz Ferdinand's fine furniture and his collection of weapons. His other obsession was landscape gardening, and the parklands and rose garden are a delight.

WHAT'S ON

May	*Prague Spring Music Festival* (mid-May): This international event consists of an array of classical music concerts in churches, palaces, and halls. It starts with a procession from Smetana's grave in the National Cemetery in Vyšehrad to the great hall named after him in the restored Obecní dům (Municipal House), where a rousing performance of his orchestral tone poem *Ma Vlast* ("*My Country*") is given.
June	*Dance Prague*: Dance festival with events at various venues, including outdoor spaces.
July/August	*Open Air Opera Festival*: The Lichtenstejnský palác (Liechtenstein Palace) hosts one of the many musical events held in historic buildings and gardens across the city.
December	*St. Nicholas* (December 5): A multitude of St. Nicks roam the streets, accompanied by an angel who rewards good children with candy and a devil who chastises appropriately. *Christmas Eve* (December 24): Live carp are sold on the streets for the traditional Czech Christmas Eve dinner. *New Year's Eve* (December 31): There are formal Sylvester balls, and, outside, crowds welcome the arrival of the New Year on the streets.

TICKETS
Tickets for events can be obtained at individual box offices (which may be cheaper) or through:

Prague Information Service   ✉ Na příkopě 20, Nové město   ☎ 2422 6097;   ✉ Old Town Hall ☎ 2448 2018

Ticketpro   ✉ Salvátorská 10, Staré město   ☎ 2481 4020 or 14051

Bohemia Ticket International   ✉ Malé náměstí 13, Staré město   ☎ 2422 7832

ENTERTAINMENT INFORMATION
The best source of information for English readers about what's on in Prague is probably the tabloid "Night and Day" section of the weekly English-language newspaper *Prague Post*. This gives listings of stage, screen, and cultural events likely to be relevant to visitors from abroad, as well as interesting reviews, comment, and analysis. Comprehensive listings of upcoming events can also be found in the monthly *Culture in Prague*.

PRAGUE's
top 25 sights

The sights are shown on the maps on the inside front cover and inside back cover, numbered **1–25** from west to east across the city

STRAHOVSKÝ KLÁŠTER

HIGHLIGHTS

- 17th-century Theological Hall
- 18th-century Philosophical Hall
- Strahovská obrazárna (Strahov Picture Gallery)
- 9th-century Strahov Gospels
- Interior of Kostel Nanebevzeti Panny Marie (Church of the Assumption)

INFORMATION

- C4
- Strahovské nádvoři 1, Hradčany
- 2051 6671
- Daily 9–noon, 1–5. Gallery: Tue–Sun 9–noon, 12:30–5
- Peklo (Hell) restaurant in monastery cellars
- Tram 22, 23 to Pohořelec
- Fair
- Moderate
- Loretánská kaple (Loretto Shrine ➤ 26), Petřin Hill (➤ 28)

Baroque spires rising toward Heaven, a gilded image of an enemy of the Faith, monks profiting from an enterprise in Hell: the hilltop Strahov Monastery seems to encapsulate something of this most paradoxical of cities.

Persuasive priests The Strahov Monastery, a major landmark in the cityscape, crowns the steep slope leading up from Malá Strana (its name derives from *strahovní*, meaning "to watch over"). It is a treasure-house of literature, and its ornate library halls with their splendid frescoes are among the most magnificent in Europe. As befits a monastery devoted to books, Strahov owed much to its abbots' way with words. Its 12th-century founder, Abbot Zdík, persuaded Prince Vladislav II to back his project by making flattering comparisons of Prague with the holy city of Jerusalem. Much later, in 1783, Abbot Meyer exercised equal powers of persuasion on Emperor Joseph II to exempt Strahov from the reforming ruler's edict that closed down many of the Habsburg Empire's monasteries. The canny cleric was so eloquent that Strahov actually benefited from the misfortune of other institutions: Books from the suppressed monastery at Louka were brought here by the wagonload. A gilded medallion of the emperor over the library entrance may also have helped to persuade Joseph that the Strahov monks deserved special treatment.

Returnees' revenge The monks, who belong to the Premonstratensian Order, were chased out of Strahov by the Communists in 1952, but have now come back. They have made the upper floor of the cloisters into a gallery for the works of art since returned to them and converted the cellars into a restaurant called Peklo (Hell).

Nový Svět

Chambermaids and scullions, footmen and flunkies—these were among the folk for whom the humble homes of Nový Svět ("New World") were originally erected back in the 14th century. The area is now more upscale.

Wizards and weird doings Nový Svět, a mysterious place of crooked alleyways and secret gardens hidden behind high walls, has never been in the city's mainstream. Castle servants lived here. So did intellectuals and others who served the masters of the castle—the Danish astronomer Tycho Brahe and his German colleague Johannes Kepler, both employed by Rudolph II to investigate the more arcane secrets of the universe.

La Bohème Today's residents are artists and writers, who have colonized the 18th-century houses along this charming cobbled street that wobbles its way westward just uphill from the castle. The painter's studio at No. 19 is crammed with pictures of curvaceous girls and grimacing gnomes, while the Czech master of animated film, Jan Švankmajer, a long-time resident, runs a gallery devoted to Surrealist art.

Connecting the worlds Nový Svět is linked to the outside world by short streets (Černínská, Kapucínská, U Kasáren, and Kanovnická) that run down the hill from the main tourist trail between Strahovský klášter and the castle, and by flights of steps that lead from the old ramparts, whose course is followed by today's trams 22 and 23.

HIGHLIGHTS

- Nepomuk statue in Černínská Street
- Birthplace of violinist F. Ondříček at No. 25
- Tycho Brahe's house at No. 1
- Church of St. John Nepomuk
- No. 3, the president's favorite restaurant

INFORMATION

- C4
- ✉ Nový Svět, Hradčany
- 🍴 Restaurant at No. 3
- 🚊 Tram 22, 23 to Brusnice
- ♿ Few
- ↔ Loretánská kaple (Loretto Shrine ► 26)

St. John Nepomuk

3

LORETÁNSKÁ KAPLE

Loretto Shrine, Hradčany

INFORMATION

- ✚ C4
- ✉ Loretánské náměstí, Hradčany
- ☎ 2051 6740
- 🕓 Tue–Sun 9–12:15, 1–4:30
- 🚋 Tram 22, 23 to Pohořelec
- ♿ Few
- 💵 Moderate
- ↔ Strahovský klášter (➤ 24), Nový Svět (➤ 25)

A bearded lady, skeletons rattling their bones to the sound of chiming bells, severed breasts on display, and a flying house are not part of a freak show, but instead are all features of the sumptuous Loretto Shrine, high up on Hradčany Hill.

Counter-Reformation fireworks No showman's trick was spared to bring the wayward Czechs back into the Catholic fold after their long flirtation with Protestantism was brought to an end by the Battle of the White Mountain in 1620. Protestant austerity, with its repudiation of images, was replaced by the idolatry of the cult of the Virgin Mary, dripping with sensuality and symbolism. Of all the flights of architectural fantasy that the Roman Catholic Counter-Reformation perpetrated on Prague, the Loretto is the most bizarre as well as the most beautiful, its church and courtyard a theater of cults, miracles, and mysteries designed to dazzle doubters and skeptics.

Weird wonders The kernel of the complex is a Santa Casa, a facsimile of the Virgin Mary's holy home in Nazareth, supposedly flown by angels from the Holy Land and deposited at Loreta in Italy. Fifty such shrines were once scattered around the Czech countryside, but this is far and away the most important, an ornate little Renaissance pavilion built in 1631 and later given an equally ornate baroque setting of courtyard, carillon tower, and richly decorated church. Pilgrims once flocked here in huge numbers to marvel at the macabre: St. Agatha offering up her bloody bosom to the angels; the skeletons in their wax death masks; unhappy St. Starosta, whose father killed her in a fury on finding she'd grown a beard to discourage a favored suitor.

ŠTERNBERSKÝ PALÁC

Who would guess that the unpretentious little alley beside the Prague archbishop's palace on Hradčanské náměstí would lead to one of the nation's great art collections? Housed in the grand Šternberg Palace, it dazzles visitors with its Old Masters.

Ambitious aristocrats Having built the Trojský zámek (Troja Château ► 48) on the edge of Prague, Count Šternberg, one of the city's richest men, needed a town house closer to Prague Castle. The Italian architect Giovanni Alliprandi was commissioned to design the palace, and work began on the count's Hradčany home in 1698. However, the money ran out before the completion of the main facade, the principal purpose of which was to upstage his neighbor, the archbishop. The interior was decorated with fine ceiling and wall paintings. It was a later Šternberg who donated much of the family's great picture collection to the fledgling National Gallery in the early 19th century, and the nation's finest foreign paintings were housed here from 1814 to 1871. They are once more in this grand setting.

Picture palace Despite being tucked away behind Hradčanské náměstí, the Šternberg Palace is an edifice of some substance, arranged around an imposing courtyard, with grand stairways and an oval pavilion facing the garden. The National Gallery of European Art attracts a stream of tourists—as well as art thieves, tempted by security that was laughably lax until it was tightened up not long ago. The pictures could keep an art lover busy for a whole day or more, though some star exhibits are no longer on view: A policy of restitution has returned them to the owners from whom they were confiscated by the Communists.

HIGHLIGHTS

- Triptych of the *Adoration of the Magi*, Giertgen tot Sint Jans
- *Adam and Eve*, Cranach
- *Feast of the Rosary*, Dürer
- *Scholar in his Study*, Rembrandt
- *Head of Christ*, El Greco
- Portraits from 2nd-century Egypt
- *Beheading of St. Dorothy*, Hans Baldung Grien
- *Eleonora of Toledo*, Bronzino
- *St. Jerome*, Ribera

INFORMATION

- ✚ C4
- ✉ Hradčanské náměstí 15, Hradčany
- ☎ 2051 4595
- ⏰ Tue–Sun 10–6
- 🍴 Café
- 🚊 Tram 22, 23 to Pražský hrad
- ♿ Few
- 💲 Moderate
- ↔ Pražský hrad (Prague Castle ► 29) Švarcenberský palác (► 54)

Top: Big Lunch, painted by Georg Flegel in 1638

5

PETŘÍN

INFORMATION

- ✚ C–D4–5
- ⊙ Rozhledna: Apr–Aug: daily 10–7. Sep–Oct: daily 10–6. Nov–Mar: Sat–Sun 10–5. Mirror Maze: Apr–Aug: daily 10–7. Sep–Oct: daily 10–6. Nov–Mar: Sat–Sun 10–5. Observatory: hours vary; for information call PIS (☎ 54 44 44)
- 🍴 Restaurant and café
- 🚟 Funicular railway, Újezd in Malá Strana
- 🚋 Tram 22, 23 to Pohořelec then walk
- ♿ Few
- 💵 Rozhledna, Mirror Maze, Observatory: inexpensive
- ↔ Strahovský klášter (Strahov Monastery ► 24)

When the press of the crowd on Charles Bridge becomes too much and the sidewalks become too hard, there's always the glorious green of Petřín Hill, its orchards and woodlands a cool retreat from the city center—and a real breath of the countryside in the metropolis.

A train with a view In 1891, for the city's great Jubilee Expo that celebrated the achievements of the Czech provinces when they still formed part of the Austrian Empire, the city fathers provided a jolly little funicular railway (the "Lanovka") to the top of Petřín Hill. Now restored, it once again carries passengers effortlessly up the steep slope. At the top there's an array of attractions, including the Rozhledna ("Lookout"), the little brother of the Eiffel Tower, also built in 1891. Its 299 steps lead to a viewing platform; some claim to have seen, on a clear day, not only the Czech Republic's Giant Mountains, 90 miles to the northeast, but also the Alps, even farther away to the southwest. And all of Prague is at your feet.

Country matters With its woods and orchards (splendid with blossom in spring), the Petřín provides a welcome counterpoint to the busy castle area. Once there were vineyards on the

hill, but these didn't survive the Thirty Years War in the 17th century. They were replaced by the superb gardens that link the palaces of Malá Strana to the surrounding hillside parklands.

PRAŽSKÝ HRAD

The thousand windows of Prague Castle gaze down into every corner of the city. This is the citadel of the Czech nation, the holder of its collective memory. It is a place of palaces, churches, streets, squares, and alleyways, a city within a city, sheltering some of the country's greatest treasures.

Age-old stronghold The princes of Prague first built a fortress on the limestone spur high above the Vltava in the 9th century, and the Czech provinces have been ruled from here ever since (except when rulers preferred to live in a long-vanished palace downtown or on the summit of the rock upstream at Vyšehrad). Every age has left its imprint on the castle; it is a storehouse of architectural styles, ranging from the foundations of Romanesque churches a thousand years old to Professor Plečnik's premature postmodernism of the interwar years. Even now, a committee is hard at work adapting the ancient complex in an attempt to make it more inviting and accessible to the citizens of a new and democratic order.

Castle denizens Teeming with tourists, the castle's courtyards also echo with the tread of countless ghosts: Emperor Charles IV, with his dreams of Prague as a great imperial capital; the cranky Habsburg ruler Rudolph II, attended by his retinue of alchemists and necromancers, soothsayers, and erotic painters; the Protestant mob that flung the hated Catholic councillors down from the Chancellery windows; Tomáš Masaryk, philosopher-president and creator of Czechoslovakia; Adolf Hitler *Heil*-ing his hysterical helots; and, most recently, the Communists, enjoying their privileges while they lasted.

HIGHLIGHTS

- Giants guarding western gateway
- Mihulka Tower
- Vladislav Hall in Old Royal Palace
- Tiny houses in Golden Lane
- Lobkovic Palace (History Museum)
- Outline of Matthias Gate in First Courtyard
- Second Courtyard, with Holy Rood Chapel and the Picture Gallery
- Third Courtyard, with statue of St. George
- Plečnik's canopy and stairway to gardens
- Riders' Staircase in Old Royal Palace

INFORMATION

- ✚ C–D4
- ✉ Pražský hrad, Hradčany
- ☎ 2437 3368
- ⊙ Courtyards and streets: daily until late. Buildings: Apr–Oct: daily 9–5. Nov–Mar: daily 9–4
- 🍴 Cafés and restaurants
- Ⓜ Malostranská, then an uphill walk
- 🚊 Tram 22, 23 to Pražský hrad
- ♿ Few
- 💵 Moderate
- ↔ Šternberský palác (➤ 27), Katedrála sv. Vita (St. Vitus's Cathedral ➤ 30)

29

KATEDRÁLA SV. VÍTA

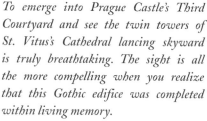

HIGHLIGHTS

- South Portal, with 14th-century mosaic
- St. Wenceslas's Chapel
- Crypt, with royal tombs
- Silver tomb of St. John Nepomuk
- West front sculptures

INFORMATION

- ✚ C/D4
- ✉ Pražský hrad, Hradčany
- 🕐 Apr–Oct: daily 9–5. Nov–Mar: daily 9–4. Tower: Apr–Oct: daily 10–5
- 🍴 Restaurants and cafés in castle
- 🚊 Tram 22, 23 to Pražský hrad (Prague Castle)
- ♿ Fair
- 💰 Newer section: free. Gothic section: moderate
- ↔ Pražský hrad (➤ 29)

Tomb of St. John Nepomuk

To emerge into Prague Castle's Third Courtyard and see the twin towers of St. Vitus's Cathedral lancing skyward is truly breathtaking. The sight is all the more compelling when you realize that this Gothic edifice was completed within living memory.

Spanning the centuries The cathedral was begun by Emperor Charles IV in the mid-14th century. It is built over the foundations of much earlier predecessors: a round church erected by "Good King" (actually Prince) Wenceslas in the early 10th century and a big Romanesque building resembling the present-day Bazilika sv. Jiří (➤ 31). The glory of the architecture is largely due to the great Swabian builder Petr Parléř and his sons, who worked on the building for 60 years. Progress was halted abruptly by the troubles of the 15th century, and the cathedral consisted only of an east end until the formation of an "Association for the Completion of the Cathedral," in 1843. Decades of effort saw the nave, western towers, and much else brought to a triumphant conclusion; in 1929, a thousand years after Prince Wenceslas was assassinated, the cathedral was consecrated, dedicated to the country's patron saint, St. Vitus.

Cathedral treasures The cathedral is a treasure-house of Bohemian history, though the Crown Jewels, its greatest prize, are seldom on display. The spacious interior absorbs the crowds with ease and provides a fitting context for an array of precious artifacts that range from medieval paintings to modern glass.

8

BAZILIKA A KLÁŠTER SV. JIŘÍ

A blood-red baroque facade conceals a severe ancient interior, the Romanesque Basilica of St. George. The nuns have long since left their convent to the north, which is now a setting for fine collections of Czech Renaissance and baroque painting and sculpture.

Bare basilica The basilica is the biggest church of its date in the Czech provinces and its twin towers and pale, sober stonework are a reminder of the great antiquity of the Prague Castle complex. Very well preserved, it is no longer used as a church but is instead a concert venue. The austere interior, a great hall with wooden ceiling, houses a small but impressive collection of artworks.

Paintings and princesses Founded in 973, St. George's Convent was a prestigious institution, a place to which princesses and other young ladies of noble birth were sent to receive the best possible education. Shut down like many other religious houses in 1782 by Emperor Joseph (who turned it into a barracks), it had to await the coming of the Communists for its rehabilitation; they planned to turn it into a Museum of the Czechoslovak People. It now houses Mannerist, baroque, and rococo painting and sculpture from the National Gallery's Old Bohemian collection. The comparatively small Mannerist holdings complement those at Obrazárna (the Prague Castle Picture Gallery ► 52). The finest artworks here represent the Bohemian baroque, which flowered at a time when Czechs were allowed few creative outlets other than the visual arts. Massive sculpted saints writhe in ecstatic frenzy. Meanwhile, secular portraits and genre scenes illustrate other sides of Bohemian life.

HIGHLIGHTS

Basilica
● Gothic tomb of Prince Vratislav I
● St. Ludmila's chapel with frescoes
● Renaissance south portal

Gallery
● Baroque Annunciation sculptures from East Bohemia
● Religious statuary by Jiří František Pacák and M.B. Braun
● *Tobias Restoring his Father's Sight* by Petr Brandl
● Landscapes by Roelandt Savery
● Genre scenes by Norbert Grund

INFORMATION

✚ D4
✉ Jiřské náměstí, Hradčany
☎ 5732 0536
🕐 Basilica: Apr–Oct: daily 9–5. Nov–Mar: daily 9–4. Gallery: Tue–Sun 10–6
🍴 Restaurants and cafés in castle
Ⓜ Malostranská, then an uphill walk
🚊 Trams 22, 23 to Pražský hrad (Prague Castle)
♿ Few
💰 Moderate
🔁 Pražský hrad (► 29)

9

NERUDOVA

HIGHLIGHTS

INFORMATION

- C–D4
- Nerudova, Malá Strana
- Restaurants and cafés
- Trams 12, 22, 23 to Malostranské náměstí (Malá Strana Square)
- Few
- Pražský hrad (Prague Castle ➤ 29)
  Chrám sv. Mikuláše (St. Nicholas's Church), Malá Strana (➤ 33)

Toil up to the castle from Malostranské náměstí (Malá Strana Square) via steep, cobbled Neruda Street and you are rewarded by a sequence of exquisite town houses, baroque and rococo, on medieval foundations, with elaborate house signs.

Eagles and other emblems It is the elegant facades and their emblems that catch the eye. There's an Eagle, Three Little Fiddles, a Goblet, a Golden Key, and a Horseshoe. The Two Suns indicate the house (No. 47) of author Jan Neruda (1843–91), who gave his name to the street; he was the Dickens of Malá Strana, a shrewd observer of the everyday life of the area. Most of the people who lived here were prosperous burghers, but some were aristocrats, like the Morzins who built their palace at No. 5 (the muscular Moors holding up the balcony are a pun on the family name). Their home is now an embassy, as is the Thun-Hohensteins' palace at No. 20; here the Moors' job is being carried out by a pair of odd-looking eagles.

Spur Street The secret of savoring Neruda Street to the full is to coast gently downward, like the coachmen from whom the road derived its earlier German name of Spornergasse (Spur Street), the spur in this case being the skid-like brake that slowed their otherwise precipitous progress down the steep slope.

The Three Little Fiddles, No. 12 Nerudova

10

CHRÁM SV. MIKULÁŠE, MALÁ STRANA

As you explore the base of the lofty St. Nicholas's Church, you feel the full power of the Catholic Counter-Reformation expressing itself in what is one of the boldest and most beautiful baroque buildings of Central Europe.

Counter-Reformation citadel When the Jesuits came to Prague following the rout of the Protestants at the Battle of the White Mountain, the existing little 13th-century church at the center of Malostranské náměstí (Malá Strana Square) was far too modest for their aspirations. The new St. Nicholas's Church was eventually completed in the 18th century, and with its lofty walls and high dome and bell tower, became one of the dominant features of the city. The Jesuits intended their church to impress, but not through size alone. They employed the finest architects of the day (the Dientzenhofers, father and son, plus Anselmo Lurago), along with the most talented interior designers. The subtly undulating west front is adorned with statues proclaiming the triumph of the Jesuit Order under the patronage of the imperial House of Habsburg. Inside, no effort was spared to enthrall via the dynamic play of space, statuary, and painting, a fantastically decorated pulpit, and a 2,500-pipe organ (played by Mozart on several occasions).

Princely palaces and humbler households In front of the huge church swirls the life of Malá Strana—locals waiting for the trams mixing with tourists following the Royal Way (▶ 16) up to Hradčany. Malostranské náměstí is lined with a fascinating mixture of ancient town houses and grand palaces, while attached to St. Nicholas's is the Jesuits's college, now part of the university.

HIGHLIGHTS

Chrám sv. Mikuláše
● West front
● St. Barbara's Chapel
● Organ with fresco of St. Cecilia
● Dome with Holy Trinity fresco
● Huge sculptures of four Church Fathers
● Trompe-l'oeil ceiling fresco by Kracker

Malostranské náměstí
● Arcaded houses
● No. 10, Renaissance house
● No. 13, Lichtenstejnský palác of 1791
● Nos. 18 and 19, Smiřický Palace and Šternberg House

INFORMATION

✚ D4
✉ Malostranské náměstí
🕐 Apr–Sep: daily 9–5.
    Oct–Mar: daily 9–4
🍴 Restaurants and cafés in square
Ⓜ Malostranská
🚊 Tram 12, 22, 23 to Malostranské náměstí
♿ Few
Ⓤ Inexpensive
↔ Nerudova (▶ 32), Valdštejnský palác (▶ 34), Karlův most (Charles Bridge ▶ 35)

11

VALDŠTEJNSKÝ PALÁC

Think of Wallenstein Palace—Prague's biggest palace—as an awful warning to eschew excessive ambition and arrogance of the kind shown by its builder, Albrecht von Wallenstein, whose aspirations to power and fame led to his assassination.

Greedy generalissimo Wallenstein's huge late Renaissance/early baroque palace crouches at the foot of Prague Castle as if waiting greedily to gobble it up. A whole city block, previously occupied by a couple of dozen houses and a brickworks, was demolished to make way for the complex of five courtyards, a barracks, a riding school, and a superb garden that were intended to reflect Wallenstein's wealth and status. Wallenstein (Valdštejn in Czech) turned the troubled early 17th century to his advantage. Having wormed his way into the emperor's favor, he became governor of Prague, then duke of Friedland. He married for money (twice), and great tracts of land (even whole towns) fell into his hands following the Battle of the White Mountain in 1620. His fortunes grew further as he quartermastered the imperial armies as well as leading them. Rightly suspicious of his subject's intentions—Wallenstein was negotiating with the enemy at the time—the emperor had him killed.

The general's garden The great hall of the palace, with its ceiling painting of Wallenstein as Mars, the god of war, can only be seen if you have friends in the Czech Senate, which now occupies the building. The formal garden is more freely accessible. The latter is dominated by the superb Sala Terrena loggia, modeled on those in Italy, and has convincing copies of the statues stolen by Swedish soldiers during the Thirty Years War.

KARLŮV MOST

Any time is right to visit Charles Bridge, the magnificent medieval crossing over the River Vltava. Enjoy the hucksters, then savor the almost sinister dusk, when sculpted saints atop the parapets gesticulate against the darkening sky.

Gothic overpass For centuries Karlův most was Prague's only bridge, built on the orders of Emperor Charles IV in the 14th century. It's a triumph of Gothic engineering, with 16 massive sandstone arches carrying it more than 1,600 feet from the Old Town to soar across Kampa Island and the Vltava River to touch down near the heart of Malá Strana. It is protected by sturdy timber cutwaters and guarded at both ends by towers; the eastern face of the Old Town Bridge Tower is richly ornamented. Its opposite number is accompanied by a smaller tower, once part of the earlier Judith Bridge.

Starry saint Charles Bridge has always been much more than a river crossing. Today's traders succeed earlier merchants and stallholders, and tournaments, battles, and executions have all been held on the bridge. The heads of the Protestants executed in 1621 in Old Town Square were displayed here. Later that century the bridge was beautified with baroque sculptures, including the statue of St. John Nepomuk. Falling foul of the king, this unfortunate cleric was pushed off the bridge in a sack. As his body bobbed in the water, five stars danced on the surface. Nepomuk hence became the patron saint of bridges, and is always depicted with his starry halo.

HIGHLIGHTS

- Old Town Bridge Tower
- Malá Strana Bridge Tower (viewpoint)
- Nepomuk statue with bronze relief panels
- Bruncvík (Roland column) to southwest
- Statue of St. John of Matha
- Bronze crucifix with Hebrew inscription
- Statue of St. Luitgard (by Braun)

INFORMATION

- ✚ D4
- 🚇 Staroměstská
- 🚊 Tram 12, 22, 23 to Malostranské náměstí
- ♿ Good
- ↔ Chrám sv. Mikuláše (St. Nicholas's Church), Malá Strana (▶ 33)

St. Anthony of Padua

NÁRODNÍ DIVADLO

HIGHLIGHTS

- Bronze troikas above the entrance loggia
- Star-patterned roof of the dome
- Frescoes in the foyer by Mikoláš Aleš
- Painted ceiling of the auditorium, by František Ženíšek
- Painted stage curtain by Vojtěch Hynais
- View of the theater from Střelecký Island
- Any performance of an opera from the Czech repertoire

INFORMATION

- ✚ D/E5
- ✉ Národní 2, Nové město
- ☎ 2490 1448
- 🍴 Bar
- Ⓜ Národní třída
- ♿ Few
- 🎭 Opera tickets: Kč40–Kč750
- ↔ Betlémská kaple (➤ 55)

A reflection of the National Theater

Even if the thought of a classical play performed in Czech doesn't enthrall you, don't miss the National Theater. It is, perhaps, the greatest of Prague's collective works of art, decorated by the finest artists of the age.

National drama Theater in Prague still spoke with a German voice in the mid-19th century. Money to build a specifically Czech theater was collected from 1849 onward, without support from German-dominated officialdom. The foundation stone was laid in 1868 with much festivity, then in 1881, just before the first performance, the theater burned down. Undiscouraged, the populace rallied, and by 1883 it had been completely rebuilt. The opening was celebrated with a grand gala performance of the opera *Libuše* by Smetana, a passionate supporter of the theater project.

Expanded ambition The National Theater stands at the New Town end of Most Legií (Legions Bridge), its bulk carefully angled to fit into the streetscape and not diminish the view to Petřín Hill on the far bank. It was given a long-deserved restoration in time for its centenary, and when it reopened in 1983 it had gained a piazza and three annexes, whose architecture has been much maligned, the least unkind comment being that the buildings seem to be clad in bubble-wrap. The city's popular multimedia show Laterna Magika (➤ 79) performs in one of these buildings, the Nová scéna.

14

UMĚLECKOPRŮMYSLOVÉ MUZEUM

Don't be put off by the uninviting building or the forlornly flapping banner of the Decorative Arts Museum. At the top of a steep flight of stairs are little-visited treasure chambers full of fine furniture, glass, porcelain, clocks, metalwork, and more.

Riverside reclaimed Looking something like a miniature Louvre, the Decorative Arts Museum was built in 1901 in an area that, by the end of the 19th century, had turned its back on the river and become a jumble of storage depots and timber yards. The city fathers decided to beautify it with fine public buildings and riverside promenades on the Parisian model. The School of Arts and Crafts (1884) and the Rudolfinum concert hall and gallery (1890) preceded the museum; the University's Philosophy Building (1929), which completed the enclosure of what is now Jan Palach Square, followed it.

Decorative delights The museum's collections are incredibly rich and diverse, numbering nearly 200,000 items of international origin; only a fraction has ever been on display at any one time. The focus is on beautiful objects originating in the Czech provinces and dating from Renaissance times to the middle of the 20th century. Totally revamped displays now reveal the collections in a fascinating new light.

The 20th century The extraordinary Czech contribution to the development of 20th-century art and design has never been dealt with adequately, a situation that has been partly remedied by the opening of the Museum of Modern Art at Veletržní palác (▶ 47) in 1995.

HIGHLIGHTS

- *Pietra dura* scene of a town by Castnicci
- Beer glasses engraved with card players
- Boulle commode and cabinet
- Monumental baroque furniture by Dientzenhofer and Santini
- Meissen Turk on a rhino
- Holíč porcelain figures
- Harrachov glass
- Klášterec figurines of Prague characters
- Biedermeier cradle
- Surprise view down into the Old Jewish Cemetery

INFORMATION

- ✚ E4
- ✉ 17 listopadu 2, Staré město
- ☎ 5109 3111
- 🕐 Tue–Sun 10–6
- 🍴 Café (🕐 Mon–Fri 10–6; Sat–Sun 10:30–6)
- Ⓜ Staroměstská
- ♿ Few
- 💰 Moderate
- ↔ Staronová synagóga, Josefov (▶ 39) Starý židovský hřbitov (Old Jewish Cemetery ▶ 40)

15

VYŠEHRAD

HIGHLIGHTS

- National Cemetery graves and memorials, and the Slavín mausoleum
- St. Martin's Rotunda (Romanesque church)
- Cihelná brána (Brick Gate), with Prague Fortifications Museum
- Baroque Leopold Gate
- Ramparts walk
- Neo-Gothic Kostel sv. Petra a Pavla (Church of St. Peter and St. Paul)
- Freestanding sculptures of Libuše and other legendary figures (by Josef Václav Myslbek)

INFORMATION

- E7
- Information center: V Pevnosti, Vyšehrad. Brick Gate: Vratislavova, Vyšehrad
- Prague Fortifications Museum: Apr–Oct: daily 9:30–5:30. Nov–Mar: daily 9:30–4:30. Cemetery: Apr–Oct: daily 8–6. Nov–Mar: daily 8–4
- Restaurant
- Vyšehrad
- Trams 3, 16, 17, 21 to Výtoň then a steep uphill walk
- Fair
- Park and cemetery: free. Museum: inexpensive
- Congress Center, Vyšehrad (➤ 51)

Rising high above the River Vltava is Vyšehrad ("High Castle"), where the soothsaying Princess Libuše foresaw the founding of Prague, "a city whose splendor shall reach unto the stars," and where she married her plowman swain, Přemysl.

Romantic rock Beneath Vyšehrad's 19th-century neo-Gothic Church of St. Peter and St. Paul are the remains of a far earlier, Romanesque church that once served the royal court. But it was in the 19th century, with the rise of Romantic ideas about history and nationhood, that poets, playwrights, and painters celebrated the great fortress-rock, elaborating the story of Libuše. Most of their efforts have been forgotten, though Smetana's "Vyšehrad" part of his glorious tone-poem *Má Vlast*, still remains

Devil's Pillars, Karlach's Park

popular. The nation's great and good have been buried in the National Cemetery (or Pantheon) at Vyšehrad since the late 19th century. Smetana himself is here, and fellow composer Dvořák.

Vltava views Everyone driving along the main riverside highway has to pay homage to Vyšehrad, as the road and tram tracks twist and turn and then tunnel through the high rock protruding into the Vltava. In the 1920s the whole hilltop was turned into a public park, with wonderful views up and down the river (➤ 51).

16

STARONOVÁ SYNAGÓGA, JOSEFOV

To step down from the street through the low portal of Josefov's Old/New Synagogue is to enter another world, one that endured a thousand years until brought to a tragic end by the brutal Nazi occupation.

Ghetto memories The Old/New Synagogue stands in the heart of Josefov, the former Jewish Ghetto. Prague's Jews moved here in the 13th century; by that time they had already lived at various locations in the city for hundreds of years. High walls kept the Jews in and their Christian neighbors out, though not in 1389, when 3,000 Jews died in a vicious pogrom and the synagogue's floor ran with blood. The ghetto community produced some remarkable characters, such as Rabbi Loew—Renaissance scholar, confidant of emperors, and creator of that archetypal man-made monster, the Golem. Molded from river mud, the mournful Golem first served his master dutifully, but eventually ran amok until the rabbi managed to calm him down. Legend has it that the monster's remains are hidden in the synagogue's loft. Far worse monsters marched in as the Germans annexed Czechoslovakia in 1939; by the end of World War II most of the country's Jews had perished, some in the Czech prison town of Terezín (Theresienstadt), the majority in Auschwitz.

Gothic synagogue With its pointed brick gable and atmospheric interior, the Gothic Old/New Synagogue of 1275 is the oldest building of its kind north of the Alps, a compelling reminder of the age-old intertwining of Jewish and Christian culture in Europe. It is at its most evocative when least crowded with visitors. Remember that for Prague's few remaining Jews it is not a museum but still a place of worship.

HIGHLIGHTS

- Vine carving in entrance portal
- Unconventional five-ribbed vaults
- Gothic grille of the *bimah* (pulpit)
- Rabbi Loew's seat
- Imperial banner recognizing Jewish bravery in the Thirty Years War
- Ark with foliage carving

INFORMATION

- ✚ E4
- ✉ Pařížská and Červená
- 🕐 Jan–Mar, Nov–Dec: Sun–Thu 9–4:30; Fri 9–2. Apr–Oct: Sun–Thu 9–6; Fri 9–5
- 🍴 Restaurant in Jewish Town Hall
- Ⓜ Staroměstská
- ♿ Few
- 💰 Moderate
- ↔ Uměleckoprůmyslové muzeum (Decorative Arts Museum ► 37), Old Jewish Cemetery (► 40) Staroměstské náměsti (Old Town Square ► 42)

17

STARÝ ŽIDOVSKÝ HŘBITOV

HIGHLIGHTS

Around the cemetery
- Jewish Town Hall with Hebraic clock
- Klausen Synagogue (Jewish traditions exhibit)
- Ceremonial Hall
- Pinkas Synagogue (77,297 names of Holocaust victims; pictures from Terezín)
- Spanish Synagogue
- Maisel Synagogue (Jewish history exhibit)
- Statue of Rabbi Loew on Magistrát building, Mariánské náměstí

In the cemetery
- Tombstone of Rabbi Loew (c1525–1609)
- Tombstone of Mayor Maisel (1528–1601)

INFORMATION

- E4
- Cemetery: enter through the Pinkas Synagogue, Široká 3
- Prague Jewish Museum: 231 7191
- Jewish Museum: Apr–Oct: Sun–Fri 9–6. Nov–Mar: Sun–Fri 9–4:30. Closed on Jewish holidays
- In Jewish Town Hall
- Staroměstská
- Fair
- Expensive
- Uměleckoprůmyslové muzeum (➤ 37), Staronová synagóga (➤ 39), Staroměstské náměstí (Old Town Square ➤ 42)

Just as the sunlight filtering through the tall trees is reduced to a dappled shade, so visitors' voices diminish to a hush as they contemplate the 12,000 toppling tombstones of the Old Jewish Cemetery, where as many as 80,000 people are buried.

The changing Ghetto   Over the centuries, the Jewish Ghetto, hemmed in by its walls, became intolerably crowded. By the time Emperor Joseph II gave the Jews partial emancipation toward the end of the 18th century, the Ghetto had 12,000 inhabitants, crammed together within it in increasingly sordid conditions. During the course of the 19th century many moved out to more salubrious quarters in the suburbs. Around 1900, the city fathers decided to "improve" the district, by then named Josefov ("Joseph's Town") in honor of the emperor. Most of it was flattened to make way for broad streets and boulevards, though the rococo Jewish Town Hall and a clutch of synagogues around the cemetery were spared. They survived under the German occupation, some say, because Hitler hoped to preserve what was left of the Ghetto as a "Museum of a Vanished Race." The stolen valuables of the Jewish communities of Bohemia and Moravia were brought to Prague, where some are now on display in the synagogues administered by the Prague Jewish Museum.

Solemn cemetery   The cemetery is evocative of the long centuries of Jewish life in Prague. Unable to extend it, the custodians were forced to bury the dead one on top of the other, up to 12 deep in places. The total number laid to rest here may amount to 80,000. Visitors leave wishful notes under pebbles on the more prominent tombstones (like that of Rabbi Loew ➤ 39).

ANEŽSKÝ KLÁŠTER

St. Agnes's Convent shelters in a quiet precinct of the Old Town and is Prague's most venerable Gothic complex. Once slated for destruction, the convent is now the fitting home for one of the country's greatest and most distinctive galleries.

Canonized Czech Agnes was a 13th-century princess, sister of Wenceslas I and founder of a convent of Poor Clares here. In its glory days St. Agnes's was a mausoleum for the royal family, but was sacked by the Hussites in the 15th century. In 1782, it was closed down by Joseph II, and became slum housing until city authorities decided to raze it in the 1890s, only relenting when faced with bitter public protest. The convent was slowly restored, and, in November 1989, days before the Communist regime ended, Agnes was made a saint. An auspicious omen?

Bohemian Renaissance The convent now displays the National Gallery's collection of medieval art from Czech lands and nearby. The magnificent paintings and sculptures show the extraordinary achievements made by the fine arts in Bohemia, above all during the reigns of Emperor Charles IV and his successors. Prague's court artists fused Italian, French, and Flemish influences in a manner all their own, pointing toward the late-Gothic style that flourished in Europe.

HIGHLIGHTS

- *Madonna of Vyšehrad* painting
- *Madonna and Child* sculpture from Český Krumlov
- Panel paintings by the Master of Vyšší Brod
- Portraits of saints by Master Theodoricus
- *Christ on the Mount of Olives* by the Třeboň Master
- Votive altarpiece from Zlichov
- *Madonna of Poleň*, Cranach the Elder
- Vaulted medieval cloister
- Church of St. Francis (concert hall)
- Church of the Holy Savior

INFORMATION

- ✚ E3
- ✉ U milosrdných 17, Staré město
- ☎ 2481 0628
- 🕐 Tue–Sun 10–6
- 🍴 Café
- Ⓜ Náměstí Republiky
- 🚊 Tram 17 (Právnická fakulta stop) or tram 5, 14 (Dlouhá třída stop)
- ♿ Fair
- ✋ Moderate

Musicians perform at St. Agnes's Convent

19

STAROMĚSTSKÉ NÁMĚSTÍ

HIGHLIGHTS

- Orloj (Astronomical Clock) from the 15th century (▶ 59)
- Council Hall and Clock Tower (▶ 51) of Old Town Hall
- Sgraffitoed House at the Minute dated 1611 (No. 2)
- Kostel sv. Mikuláše (the baroque Church of St. Nicholas)
- Jan Hus Memorial of 1915
- Sidewalk crosses in front of Old Town Hall
- Palác Goltz-Kinských (▶ 52)
- The Gothic Dům u Kamenného Zvonu (House at the Stone Bell)
- Renaissance house (No. 14)
- Arcaded houses Nos. 22–26, with baroque facades and medieval interiors and cellars

INFORMATION

- ✚ E4
- ✉ Staroměstské náměstí, Staré město
- 🍴 Restaurants and cafés
- Ⓜ Staroměstská
- ♿ Fair
- ↔ Staronová synagóga, Josefov (▶ 39)

Visitors throng the spacious Old Town Square at all times of year, entertained by street performers, refreshed at outdoor cafés, and enchanted by the Orloj—the Astronomical Clock—and the cheerful facades of the old buildings.

Square and Týn Church

Martyrs and mournful memories The Old Town Square has not always been so jolly. The medieval marketplace became a scene of execution where Hussites lost their heads in the 15th century and 27 prominent Protestants were put to death in 1621 (they are commemorated by white crosses in the pavement). In 1945, in a final act of spite, diehard Nazis demolished a whole wing of the Old Town Hall; the site has still not been built on. On February 25, 1948, Premier Gottwald proclaimed the triumph of Communism from the rococo Goltz-Kinský Palace.

Around the square The hub of the square is the Jan Hus Memorial, an extraordinary art-nouveau sculpture whose base is one of the few places in the square where you can sit without having to buy a drink. To your left rise the blackened towers of the Týn Church (▶ 55), while to your right is the Old Town Hall, an attractively varied assembly of buildings and, further around, the city's second St. Nicholas's Church. The fine town houses surrounding the square are a study in various architectural styles, from the genuine Gothic House at the Stone Bell to the 19th-century Gothic Revival No. 16.

VÁCLAVSKÉ NÁMĚSTÍ

Despite its sometimes rather seedy air, Wenceslas Square is still the place where the city's heart beats most strongly, and to meet someone "beneath the horse" (the Wenceslas statue) remains a special thrill.

When is a square not a square? When it's a boulevard. "Václavák," 2,300 feet long, slopes gently up to the imposing facade of the National Museum (▶ 44), which is fronted by the statue of Wenceslas on his sprightly steed. This is a good place to arrange a rendezvous—whatever the time of day there's always some action, with daytime shoppers and sightseers replaced by every species of night owl as darkness falls.

History in the making Many dramas of modern times have been played out in Wenceslas Square. The new state of Czechoslovakia was proclaimed here in 1918, and in 1939 German tanks underlined the republic's demise. In 1968, more tanks arrived—this time to crush the Prague Spring of Alexander Dubček. To protest at the Soviet occupation, Jan Palach burned himself to death here the following year, and in 1989 Dubček and Václav Havel waved from the balcony of No. 36 as half a million Czechs crowded the square to celebrate the collapse of Communism.

Museum of modern architecture The procession of buildings lining both sides of the square, from the resplendent art-nouveau Hotel Evropa (▶ 84) to the elegant Functionalist Bata Store, tells the story of the distinctively Czech contribution to 20th-century architecture and design. Even more intriguing are the arcades (*pasáž*) that burrow deep into the buildings, creating a labyrinthine world of boutiques, theaters, cafés, and movie theaters.

HIGHLIGHTS

- St. Wenceslas statue, Josef Myslbek (1912)
- Arcades of the Lucerna Palace
- Hotel Evropa, completed 1905 (No. 25)
- 1920s Functionalist Bata and Lindt buildings (Nos. 6, 12)
- Ambassador, late art-nouveau hotel of 1912 (No. 5)
- Memorial to the victims of Communism
- 1950s Soviet-style Jalta Hotel (No. 45)
- Former Bank of Moravia of 1916 (Nos. 38–40)
- Art-nouveau Peterka building of 1901 (No. 12)
- Koruna Palace of 1914 (No. 1)

INFORMATION

- ✚ E4–F5
- ✉ Václavské náměstí, Nové město
- 🍴 Many restaurants and cafés
- Ⓜ Můstek or Muzeum
- ♿ Fair
- ↔ Národní muzeum (National Museum ▶ 44)

NÁRODNÍ MUZEUM

HIGHLIGHTS

- Allegorical sculptures on the terrace
- The Pantheon and dome
- Coin collection
- Collection of precious stones
- Skeleton of a whale

INFORMATION

- ✚ F5
- ✉ Václavské náměstí 68, Nové město
- ☎ 2449 7111
- ◉ Oct–Apr: daily 9–5. May–Sep: daily 10–6. Closed first Tue of month
- 🍴 Café
- 🏛 Muzeum
- ♿ Few
- 💰 Moderate
- ↔ Václavské náměstí (Wenceslas Square ➤ 43)

Some people find Prague's National Museum disappointing, crammed as it is with cabinets full of beetles and mineral specimens. However, try to enjoy it as a period piece in its own right, for its dusty showcases are as venerable as the building itself.

Top building With its gilded dome crowning the rise at the top of Václavské náměstí (Wenceslas Square ➤ 43), Prague's National Museum provides a grand finale to the capital's most important street. The neo-Renaissance building was completed in 1891, and at the time was as much an object of pride to the Czech populace as the Národní divadlo (National Theater ➤ 36). Such is its presence that some visitors have mistaken it for the parliament building, as did the Soviet gunner who raked its facade with machine-gun fire in August 1968.

An array of -ologies Even if you are not a keen entomologist, paleontologist, zoologist, mineralogist, or numismatist, you can't fail to be impressed by the evidence assembled here of the 19th century's great passion for collecting and classifying. Perhaps more immediately attractive are the temporary exhibitions, which draw on the museum's vast collections; the dinosaur display is likely to prove compelling to young

Allegorical figure of the River Vltava, on the stairway leading up to the National Museum

visitors. Above all, the building itself is impressive, with its grand stairways, statuary, mosaics, and patterned floors. And unlike most other attractions in Prague, it's open on Mondays.

NÁRODNÍ TECHNICKÉ MUZEUM

Did you know that Czechoslovakia had one of the world's biggest auto industries and that Škoda cars are legendary for their toughness and reliability? That a horse-drawn railroad once linked Bohemia with Austria? That a Czechoslovak fleet once sailed the oceans?

Past glories The answer to all these questions will be "yes," after you've visited the wonderful National Technical Museum, off the beaten track on the edge of Letenské sady (Letná Plain). The facelessness of the building belies the richness and fascination of its contents, a celebration of the longstanding technological prowess of inventive and hard-working Czechs. The Czech provinces were the industrial power-house of the Austro-Hungarian Empire, their steel works and coal mines providing the foundation for excellence in engineering of all kinds, from the production of weapons to locomotive manufacture. Later, between the two world wars, independent Czechoslovakia's light industries led the world in innovativeness and quality.

Trains and boats and planes The museum's collection of technological artifacts is displayed to spectacular effect in the vast glass-roofed and galleried main hall, where balloons and biplanes hang in space above ranks of sinister-looking streamlined limousines and powerful steam engines. The side galleries tell the story of "The Wheel" and of navigation, from rafting timber on the Vltava to transporting ore across the oceans in the Czechoslovak carrier *Košice*. Deep underground there's an exhibit of a coal mine, and other sections tell you all you ever wanted to know about time, sound, geodesy, photography, and astronomy.

HIGHLIGHTS

- 1928 Škoda fire engine
- Laurin and Klement soft-top roadster
- President Masaryk's V-12 Tatra
- Soviet ZIS 110B limousine
- Express locomotive 375-007 of 1911
- Imperial family's railway dining car of 1891
- Bleriot XI Kašpar monoplane
- Sokol monoplane

INFORMATION

- E3
- Kostelní 42, Holešovice
- 2039 9111
- Tue–Sun 9–5
- Trams 1, 8, 18, 26 to Letenské náměstí, or Metro Vltavská then tram 1 to Letenské náměstí
- Few
- Moderate
- Veletržní palác (Museum of Modern Art ➤ 47), Letenské sady (Letná Plain ➤ 50)

OBECNÍ DŮM

HIGHLIGHTS

- Entrance canopy and mosaic *Homage to Prague*
- Smetanova síň (Smetana Hall), with frescoes symbolizing the dramatic arts
- Mayor's Suite, with paintings by Mucha
- Rieger Hall, with Myslbek sculptures
- Palacký Room, with paintings by Preisler

INFORMATION

- ✚ E/F4
- ✉ Náměstí Republiky 5, Staré město
- ☎ 2200 2100
- 🕐 Check locally
- Ⓜ Náměstí Republiky
- ♿ Few
- ↔ Kostel sv. Jakuba (➤ 55), House at the Black Madonna (➤ 56)

The prosaic name "Municipal House" fails to convey anything of the character of this extraordinary art-nouveau building, a gloriously extravagant early 20th-century confection on which every artist of the day seems to have left his stamp.

City council citadel Glittering like some gigantic, flamboyant jewel, more brightly than ever since its restoration in 1997, the Obecní dům is linked to the blackened Prašná brána (Powder Tower ➤ 50), last relic of the Old Town's fortifications and long one of the city's main symbols. The intention of the city fathers in the first years of the 20th century was to add an even more powerful element to the cityscape that would celebrate the glory of the Czech nation and Prague's place within it. The site of the old Royal Palace was selected, and no expense was spared to erect a megastructure in which the city's burgeoning life could expand.

Ornamental orgy The building program included meeting and assembly rooms, cafés, restaurants, bars, even a pâtisserie, while the mayor was provided with particularly luxurious quarters. The 1,149-seat Smetana Hall, home of the Prague Symphony Orchestra, is a temple to the muse of Bohemian music. Everything is encrusted with lavish decoration, in stucco, glass, mosaic, murals, metalwork, and textiles.

The glittering portal of the Obecní dům

VELETRŽNÍ PALÁC

"A truly great experience was a tour of the Prague Trades Fair Building. The first impression... is breathtaking." So enthused the architect Le Corbusier in 1928, shortly after this monumental structure, now the Museum of Modern Art, was completed.

Trailblazer Never lacking in ego, the great master builder and design pioneer Le Corbusier was none the less vexed to find that his Czech colleagues had got in first in completing what is one of the key buildings in the evolution of 20th-century design, a secular, modern-day cathedral constructed in concrete, steel, and glass. Set in the suburb of Holešovice, the palace was intended to be a showpiece for the products of Czechoslovakia. However, trade fairs moved away from Prague to Brno, and for many years the great building languished in neglect and obscurity, its originality forgotten as its architectural innovations became the norm throughout the world.

Disguised blessing After fire gutted the palace in 1974, it was decided to use its elegant spaces to display the National Gallery's modern art treasures, which had previously been hidden away without a proper home. In all, it took around 20 years to complete the restoration work. Now the engrossing Czech 19th-century collection leads the way to the amazing achievements of Czech painters and sculptors in the early part of the 20th century. The museum also shows works by the French Impressionists and other modern foreign art. Among the paintings on display are *Self-portrait*, by Picasso, and Van Gogh's *Green Rye*. The museum promotes contemporary arts of all types, staging the kind of major international art shows of which the Czechs were so long deprived.

HIGHLIGHTS

- *Winter Evening in Town*, Jakub Schikaneder
- *Reader of Dostoyevsky*, Emil Filla
- *Serie C VI*, František Kupka
- *Melancholy*, Jan Zrzavý
- *Sailor*, Karel Dvořák
- *Self-portrait*, Picasso
- *Self-portrait*, Douanier Rousseau
- *Green Rye*, Van Gogh
- *Virgin*, Gustav Klimt
- *Pregnant Woman and Death*, Egon Schiele

INFORMATION

- ✚ F2
- ✉ Dukelských hrdinů 47, Holešovice
- ☎ 2430 1111
- 🕐 Tue–Wed, Fri–Sun 10–6; Thu 10–9
- 🍴 Café
- Ⓜ Vltavská
- 🚊 Tram 5 from Náměstí Republiky
- ♿ Good
- 💰 Moderate
- ↔ Národní technické muzeum (National Technical Museum ➤ 45)

Top: Green Rye, *by Van Gogh*

47

25

TROJSKÝ ZÁMEK

INFORMATION

Out here you can catch a glimpse of how delightful Prague's countryside must have been three centuries ago, with vine-clad slopes, trees in abundance, plus the resplendent baroque palace Troja Château among the allées and parterres.

Prague's Versailles This extravagant palace was built not by the monarch, but by the second richest man in Prague, Count Wenceslas Adelbert Šternberg. The Šternbergs profited from the Thirty Years War, and at the end of the 17th century were in a position to commission Jean-Baptiste Mathey to design a country house along the lines of the contemporary châteaux of the architect's native France. The south-facing site by the river, oriented directly on St. Vitus's Cathedral and Prague Castle on the far side of the Royal Hunting Grounds, now Stromovka Park, was ideal for Šternberg, allowing him to offer the monarch the right kind of hospitality following a day's hunting.

Ornamental extravagance The palace's proportions are grandiose, and its painted interiors go over the top in paying homage to the country's Habsburg rulers. And over the top, too, goes a turbaned Turk as he topples, in stunning trompe l'oeil, from the mock battlements in the grand hall. Troja was acquired by the state in the 1920s, but restored only in the late 1980s (some think excessively). It contains part of Prague's collection of 19th-century paintings, few of which can compete with the flamboyance of their setting.

Troja's grounds abound in ornamentation

PRAGUE's
best

PANORAMAS

Across the river

Some of the finest views of Prague are those in which the city is seen across the broad waters of the Vltava, as from the Smetana statue or Kampa Island. A stroll along the embankments and footpaths on both sides of the river is equally rewarding, as are the islands—Slovanský ostrov (Slavonic Island) and Střelecký ostrov (Shooters' Island).

Malá Strana from Petřín

EMBANKMENT, KAMPA ISLAND

From the shady parkland of Kampa Island there is an unusual view across the Vltava over Karlův most (Charles Bridge) and the weir to the Old Town.

🔲 D4 ✉ U Sovových mlýnů 🕐 Permanently open 🚊 Trams 12, 22, 23 to Hellichova 💷 Free

KATEDRÁLA SV. VÍTA (TOWER, ST. VITUS'S CATHEDRAL)

Climb the 287 steps of St. Vitus's Cathedral tower for one of the best panoramas of the city, and close-ups of the cathedral (▶ 30), with its bristling buttresses, diamond-tiled roofs, and copper cockerels.

🔲 C/D4 ✉ Pražský hrad 🕐 Apr–Oct: daily 10–5 🍴 Cafés and restaurants 🚊 Trams 22, 23 to Pražský hrad 💷 Inexpensive

LETENSKÉ SADY (LETNÁ PLAIN)

These parks and gardens stretch from the eastern end of Prague Castle (▶ 29), high above the banks of the Vltava. Between 1955 and 1962 a monster statue of Stalin stood here. The plinth, now infested with skateboarders, is occupied by a giant metronome, and makes an excellent vantage point over the river.

🔲 D–E3 ✉ Letenské sady 🕐 Always accessible 🚇 Malostranská and uphill walk 🚊 Tram 18 to Chotkovy sady or 22, 23 to Královský letohrádek 💷 Free

PRAŠNÁ BRÁNA (POWDER TOWER)

The sumptuous roofscape of the adjoining Obecní dům (Municipal House ▶ 46) makes an immediate impact, but this panorama is particularly appealing because of the vista along Celetná Street into the heart of the Old Town.

🔲 E/F4 ✉ Náměstí Republiky 🕐 Mar–Oct: daily 10–6 🚇 Náměstí Republiky 🚊 Trams 5, 14 to Náměstí Republiky 💷 Inexpensive

ROZHLEDNA (PETŘÍN HILL LOOKOUT TOWER)

This little brother of the Eiffel Tower was erected for Prague's great Jubilee Expo of 1891. Prepare to climb 299 steps.

🔲 C4 ✉ Petřín 🕐 Apr–Aug: daily 10–7. Sep–Oct: daily 10–6. Nov–Mar: Sat–Sun 10–5 🚊 Tram 12, 22, 23 to Hellichova, then Lanovka funicular (from Újezd) 💷 Inexpensive

SMETANA STATUE

The walkway leading to the Muzeum Bedřicha Smetany (the Smetana Museum ▶ 57) is in fact a pier (known as Novotného lávka), built out into the river. At its very tip are café tables and a statue of the composer; the view across the river, whose roaring weir drowns all intrusive noises, is the classic one of Charles Bridge, Malá Strana, and Prague Castle above.

➕ D4 ✉ Novotného lávka ⏰ Always open 🍴 Café and restaurant 🚇 Staroměstská 🚊 Trams 17, 18 to Karlovy lázně 👤 Free

STAROMĚSTSKÁ RADNICE (TOWER, OLD TOWN HALL)

The climb, on foot or by elevator, up the tower of the Old Town Hall is well worthwhile for the dizzying view it gives of the swarming activity in Old Town Square (▶ 42), as well as of the higgledy-piggledy red-tiled roofs of the medieval Old Town.

➕ E4 ✉ Staroměstské náměstí ☎ 2448 3254 ⏰ Apr–Sep: Mon 11–6; Tue–Sun 9–6. Oct–Mar: Mon 11–5; Tue–Sun 9–5 🍴 Restaurants in square 🚇 Staroměstská 👤 Moderate

STARÝ KRÁLOVSKÝ PALÁC (OLD ROYAL PALACE)

After admiring the interiors of the Old Royal Palace and the Vladislav Hall, take a stroll on the south-facing terrace or peep through the windows from which the Catholic councillors were thrown out in 1618 (▶ 12). All Prague lies at your feet.

➕ D4 ✉ Pražský hrad ☎ 2437 3368 ⏰ Apr–Oct: daily 9–5. Nov–Mar: daily 9–4 🍴 Cafés and restaurants 🚊 Tram 22, 23 to Pražský hrad 👤 Moderate

TELEVIZNÍ VYSÍLAČ (TELEVISION TOWER)

This immense television transmitter tower in the inner suburb of Žižkov, 709 feet tall, may be a blot on Prague's townscape, but its gallery does give visitors stupendous views over the city and its surroundings. The best time to take the elevator to the top is fairly early in the day, before the sun has moved too far around to the west.

➕ G5 ✉ Mahlerovy sady ☎ 6700 5784 ⏰ Daily 10AM–11PM 🍴 Restaurant 🚇 Jiřího z Poděbrad 🚊 Trams 5, 9, 26 to Lipanská 👤 Moderate

VYŠEHRAD

A walk around the ramparts of the old fortifications of Vyšehrad gives contrasting views along the Vltava far below. Upstream, Prague is surprisingly countrified, with rough woodland and rugged limestone crags, while downstream the panorama reveals the city, especially Hradčany, from an entirely new angle. Nearby, the terraces of the Communists' huge Palace of Culture (now the Congress Center) offer a view across the deep Nusle ravine toward the New Town, guarded by the walls of the Karlov Monastery.

➕ E6/7 ✉ Vyšehrad ⏰ Permanently accessible 🍴 Restaurant 🚇 Vyšehrad 🚊 Trams 3, 7, 17 to Výtoň

Old Town Square from the Old Town Hall tower

Unpopular neighbor

Building the unlovely TV tower in Žižkov necessitated destroying part of an old Jewish cemetery and was resisted by locals and other protesters (insofar as any resistance was possible in Communist days). Some people are still uneasy, claiming that they pick up transmissions on virtually any metal object, or that their bodies are being slowly microwaved.

GALLERIES

Unseen art

Housing Prague's vast and varied art collections has always posed problems. Under Communism, many pictures and other art objects were kept more or less permanently in storage, and the unique Czech contribution to 20th-century art was never properly celebrated. The big issue is now a financial one. If there are particular works you want to see, check whether they are actually on display before you make a detour to see them.

DŮM U ZLATÉHO PRSTENU (HOUSE AT THE GOLDEN RING)

The Prague City Gallery's fine collection of 20th- and 21st-century Czech art. The gallery stages large exhibitions a few steps away at the House at the Stone Bell, a Gothic tower house that restorers discovered behind a rococo facade in the 1960s.

✚ E4 ⊠ Týnská 6, Staré město ☎ 2482 7022 🕐 Tue–Sun 10–6 🍴 Cafés and restaurants 🚇 Staroměstská 💲 Moderate

LAPIDÁRIUM

Masterpieces of Czech sculpture, including some of the original statues from Karlův most (Charles Bridge ► 35), brought here for protection.

✚ F2 ⊠ Výstaviště, Holešovice ☎ 3337 5636 🕐 Tue–Fri noon–6; Sat–Sun 10–6 🍴 Restaurants and cafés in grounds 🚇 Nádraží Holešovice 🚋 Trams 5, 12, 17 to Výstaviště 💲 Inexpensive

PALÁC GOLTZ-KINSKÝCH (GOLTZ-KINSKÝ PALACE)

The National Gallery's flagship space for changing exhibitions of all kinds. It was from a balcony here that Klement Gottwald proclaimed the victory of the working classes in 1948.

✚ E4 ⊠ Staroměstské náměstí 12 ☎ 2481 0758 🕐 Tue–Sun 10–6 🍴 Cafés and restaurants in Old Town Square 🚇 Staroměstská 💲 Moderate

House at the Stone Bell

OBRAZÁRNA (PRAGUE CASTLE PICTURE GALLERY)

Mannerist and baroque paintings and sculptures, handsomely displayed, recall the fervent creative atmosphere at the castle under Rudolph II.

✚ C4 ⊠ Second Courtyard, Prague Castle, Hradčany ☎ 2437 3368 🕐 Daily 10–6 🍴 Cafés and restaurants in castle 🚋 Trams 22, 23 to Pražský hrad 💲 Moderate

MUSEUMS

BERTRAMKA (MOZART MUSEUM)

Mozart's closest friends in Prague were the Dušeks, and the Bertramka was their rural retreat. This is the place where the great composer dashed off the last lines of *Don Giovanni* before conducting its premiere in the Stavovské divadlo (Estates Theater ▶ 75).

➕ C6 ✉ Mozartova 169, Smíchov ☎ 54 38 93 🕐 Apr–Oct: daily 9:30–6. Nov–Mar: daily 9:30–5 🚇 Anděl, then Tram 4, 7, 9, 10 to Bertramka (one stop) 💷 Inexpensive

MUZEUM HLAVNÍHO MĚSTA PRAHY (CITY MUSEUM)

This pompous late 19th-century building contains exhibits telling the story of Prague's evolution from the earliest times. The star is a scale model of the city as it was in the 1820s and 1830s, meticulously put together by a person of infinite patience named Antonín Langweil. Most of the extensive collections are in storage, but selections are shown in rotation.

➕ F4 ✉ Na poříčí 52, north Nové město ☎ 2481 6772 🕐 Tue–Sun 9–6 🚇 Florenc 💷 Inexpensive

MUZEUM POLICIE ČR (POLICE MUSEUM)

This museum recovered quickly from the collapse of the old order in 1989 and gives an upbeat account of Czech policing, with plenty of gore and weaponry on show in, incongruously, what was once the Karlov Monastery.

➕ E6 ✉ Ke Karlovu 1, Nové město ☎ 29 52 09 🕐 Tue–Sun 10–5 🚇 I.P. Pavlova or Vyšehrad 💷 Inexpensive

NÁPRSTKOVO MUZEUM (NÁPRSTEK MUSEUM)

Intriguing ethnographical exhibits assembled by a 19th-century collector in love with the indigenous cultures of the Americas and Pacific.

➕ E4 ✉ Betlémské náměstí 1, Staré město ☎ 2222 1416 🕐 Tue–Sun 9–noon, 12:45–5:30 🚇 Staroměstská or Národní třída 💷 Moderate

SBÍRKA MIMOEVROPSKÉHO UMĚNÍ (ASIAN ART MUSEUM)

A magnificent baroque chateau houses the National Gallery's extensive Chinese and Japanese collections and smaller displays of Islamic and South Asian art. From downtown, it's a one-hour metro and bus ride.

➕ Off map, 8 miles south of downtown ✉ Zámek Zbraslav, Zbraslav ☎ 5792 1638 🕐 Tue–Sun 10–6 🚇 Smíchovské nádraží, then bus 129, 241, 243, 255, 360 to Zbraslavské náměstí 💷 Moderate

The big guns

Czech and Slovak involvement in the big conflict that never happened, the face-off of the Cold War, is chillingly displayed in the huge collection of military hardware on show at the Letecké muzeum (Aircraft Museum) at Kbely airfield, on the city's eastern outskirts. Some of the aircraft date back to World War I, but above all it's the Russian MiG jetfighters that remain in the memory.

More militaria

Almost unknown abroad, the tale of Czech and Slovak involvement in the conflicts of the 20th century is told in the Armádní muzeum (Army Museum) at the foot of the National Memorial in the inner suburb of Žižkov.

PALACES

Auto sculpture

In summer 1989, the streets around the West German Embassy were clogged with Wartburgs and Trabants abandoned by their East German owners. A fiberglass Trabant on mighty legs now stands in the embassy garden as a memorial to those days.

Coat of arms, Archbishop's Palace

High diplomacy

The Anglophile and athletic first president of Czechoslovakia, Tomáš Masaryk, is said to have maintained good relations with the British ambassador in the Thun Palace, on Malá Strana's tiny Thunovská street, by climbing down a ladder set against Prague Castle's walls to drop in for tea.

See Top 25 Sights for
ROYAL PALACE (► 29)
ŠTERNBERSKÝ PALÁC (► 27)
VALDŠTEJNSKÝ PALÁC (► 34)

ARCIBISKUPSKÝ PALÁC (ARCHBISHOP'S PALACE)

The lusciously restored rococo facade hides a sumptuous residence, unfortunately accessible only on special occasions.
➕ C4 ✉ Hradčanské náměstí 16, Hradčany ⏰ Not normally open to the public 🚋 Trams 22, 23 to Pražský hrad

ČERNÍNSKÝ PALÁC (ČERNÍN PALACE)

It was from this huge baroque structure (completed 1720), now the Foreign Ministry, that Jan Masaryk fell to his death in 1948.
➕ C4 ✉ Loretánské náměstí, Hradčany ⏰ Not open to the public 🚋 Tram 22, 23 to Pohořelec

DŮM PÁNŮ Z KUNŠTÁTU A PODĚBRAD (HOUSE OF THE LORDS OF KUNŠTÁT AND PODĚBRADY)

This Romanesque-Gothic mansion is possibly the most ancient interior accessible to the public. It was home to King George of Poděbrady in the 15th century.
➕ E4 ✉ Řetězová 3, Staré město ⏰ Summer: daily 11–6. Closed winter 🚇 Staroměstská 💵 Inexpensive

LOBKOVICKÝ PALÁC (LOBKOVIC PALACE)

This superb baroque structure (not to be confused with the Lobkovic Palace within the castle precinct), the residence of the German ambassador, saw strange scenes in summer 1989, when it became a temporary home to thousands of East Germans seeking refuge.
➕ C4 ✉ Vlašská 19, Malá Strana ⏰ Not open to the public 🚋 Tram 12, 22, 23 to Malostranské náměstí

SCHÖNBORNSKÝ PALÁC (SCHÖNBORN-COLLOREDO PALACE)

The U.S. Embassy occupies a baroque palace whose grandeur equals that of the nearby German Embassy.
➕ D4 ✉ Tržiště 15, Malá Strana ⏰ Not open to the public 🚋 Tram 12, 22, 23 to Malostranské náměstí

ŠVARCENBERSKÝ PALÁC (SCHWARZENBERG PALACE)

The city's most imposing Renaissance palace sits just outside Prague Castle, its sgraffito-bedecked facade and bristling gables making a noble impression. The palace houses a museum of military history.
➕ C4 ✉ Hradčanské náměstí 2, Hradčany ☎ 2020 2020 ⏰ Check locally 🚋 Trams 22, 23 to Pražský hrad 💵 Inexpensive

CHURCHES

BETLÉMSKÁ KAPLE (BETHLEHEM CHAPEL)

You must see this barn-like structure where Jan Hus preached to really appreciate the deeply nonconformist traditions so thoroughly obscured by centuries of imposed Catholicism. The chapel, in the Old Town, was completely reconstructed in the 1950s.

🔠 E4 ⊠ Betlémské náměstí, Staré město ⏰ Daily 10–5 🍴 Restaurants and cafés nearby 🚇 Národní třída 💰 Inexpensive

KOSTEL PANNY MARIE PŘED TÝNEM (TÝN CHURCH)

Among the city's best-known landmarks is the Gothic Týn Church, whose twin towers stick up spikily behind the houses east of Old Town Square. Inside are some fascinating tombs.

🔠 E4 ⊠ Týnská and Celetná, Staré město ⏰ May only be open for services due to reconstruction 🍴 Cafés and restaurants nearby 🚇 Staroměstská or Náměstí Republiky

Týn Church

KOSTEL PANNY MARIE VÍTĚZNÉ (CHURCH OF OUR LADY VICTORIOUS)

After Czech Protestantism was crushed in 1621, this church became a center of the Counter-Reformation, thanks not least to miracles wrought by the Bambino di Praga waxwork (see panel).

🔠 D4 ⊠ Karmelitská 9, Malá Strana ⏰ Mon–Sat 8:30–5:30; Sun 1–5 🚋 Tram 12, 22, 23 to Hellichova

KOSTEL SV. JAKUBA (ST. JAMES'S CHURCH)

Beneath the baroque froth is an ancient Gothic church, though you'd hardly guess it. The acoustics of the long nave are particularly impressive, and concerts held here are generally well attended.

🔠 E4 ⊠ Malá Štupartská, Staré město ⏰ Daily 9:30–4 🚇 Náměstí Republiky

KOSTEL SV. MIKULÁŠE, STARÉ MĚSTO (ST. NICHOLAS'S CHURCH, OLD TOWN)

St. Nicholas's twin towers and grand dome are the work of the great baroque architect Kilian Ignaz Dientzenhofer. His church is now a prominent feature of Old Town Square, but it was originally designed to fit into the narrow street that once ran here.

🔠 E4 ⊠ Staroměstské náměstí, Staré město ⏰ Apr–Oct: Mon noon–4; Tue–Sat 10–4; Sun noon–3. Nov–Mar: Tue, Thu, Fri, Sun 10–noon; Wed 10–4 🚇 Staroměstská

Rough justice

A withered hand hangs from the altar in St. James's Church, severed by a butcher when the thief to whom it belonged was apprehended by the Virgin Mary, who refused to let go.

Bambino di Praga

The Bambino di Praga waxwork was given to the Church of Our Lady Victorious in 1628 as part of the re-Catholicization imposed on the wayward Czechs. The miracles performed by the diminutive effigy of the infant Jesus are even more numerous than its 60 sumptuous changes of outfit.

55

TWENTIETH-CENTURY BUILDINGS

See Top 25 Sights for
OBECNÍ DŮM (MUNICIPAL HOUSE ► 46)
VELETRŽNÍ PALÁC, MUSEUM OF
    MODERN ART (► 47)

Art nouveau

The glorious effusions of art nouveau, with its use of sinuous lines and motifs from the natural world, mark the townscape all over the city. Prague rivals Vienna in the number of edifices built in this style, known here as Secession.

The famous Black Madonna

Czech innovations

Art nouveau/Secession was an international style, but later Czech architects created unique movements of their own—cubist architecture, for instance, and the intricate Rondo-Cubism that then followed.

BANKA LEGIÍ (BANK OF THE LEGIONS)
Czechoslovak legionaries fought on many fronts in World War I, and the sculptures decorating the facade of this handsome Rondo-Cubist (see panel) building of 1923 commemorate their exploits.
🞤 F4 ⊠ Na poříčí 24, north Nové město 🕓 Accessible during banking hours 🚇 Náměstí Republiky

CUBIST STREETLAMP
This extraordinary little object, an echo of Czech Cubism, still seems to vibrate with the artistic excitements that suffused metropolitan life in early 20th-century Prague.
🞤 E5 ⊠ Jungmannovo náměstí, Nové město 🚇 Můstek

DŮM U ČERNÉ MATKY BOŽÍ
(HOUSE AT THE BLACK MADONNA)
This striking example of Czech Cubist architecture, designed by Josef Gočár (1912), stands challengingly at the corner of Celetná Street in the heart of the Old Town, yet somehow manages to harmonize with its surroundings. Look for the Black Madonna in her gilded cage.
🞤 E4 ⊠ Ovocný trh 19, Staré město 🕓 Art gallery: Tue–Sun 10–6 🚇 Náměstí Republiky 🎟 Inexpensive

HLAVNÍ NÁDRAŽÍ (MAIN STATION)
Above the modern concourses rise the richly ornamented art-nouveau buildings of Prague's main station (1909), originally named after Emperor Franz Joseph, then after President Wilson.
🞤 F4 ⊠ Wilsonova 8, Nové město 🕓 24 hours 🍴 Buffet 🚇 Hlavní nádraží 🎟 Free

NOS. 7 & 9 NÁRODNÍ (NÁRODNÍ TŘÍDA)
Fascinating variations on the theme of art nouveau can be traced in the facades of these adjoining office buildings. Both were designed by Osvald Polívka; No. 9 was built for the publisher Topič and No. 7 for an insurance company.
🞤 E5 ⊠ Národní 7 & 9, Nové město 🚇 Národní třída

U NOVÁKŮ
This lavishly decorated art-nouveau structure, now a casino, was built as a department store in 1903. The colorful mosaic, by Jan Preisler, flowing over its facade, represents Trade and Industry.
🞤 E5 ⊠ Vodičkova 30, Nové město 🕓 Open to customers of Variété Praga 🍴 Restaurant 🚇 Můstek

For Music Lovers

See Top 25 Sights for
CHRÁM SV. MIKULÁŠE, MALÁ STRANA (▶ 33)
NÁRODNÍ DIVADLO
(NATIONAL THEATER) (▶ 36)

BERTRAMKA (MOZART MUSEUM ▶ 53)

DVOŘÁK'S BIRTHPLACE
Dvořák was born the son of an innkeeper in the unassuming little village of Nelahozeves on the Elbe River. His birthplace, at the foot of the Lobkovic family's huge Renaissance castle, is now a museum.
✚ Off map, about 20 miles northwest of Prague ✉ Nelahozeves 12
☎ 0205 785099 🕐 Tue–Thu, Sat, Sun 9–noon, 2–5; Fri 9–noon
🚉 Nelahozeves–zástávka (one stop after Kralupy nad Vltavou)
💰 Inexpensive

MUZEUM BEDŘICHA SMETANY
(SMETANA MUSEUM)
The museum dedicated to the composer of "Vltava" is appropriately sited in a building that rises directly out of the river.
✚ D4 ✉ Novotného lávka 1, Staré město ☎ 2422 9075
🕐 Wed–Mon 10–5 🚇 Staroměstská 💰 Inexpensive

RUDOLFINUM
Classical music lovers revere this elegant hall (▶ 76). Contemporary art buffs will find major exhibitions in the equally beautiful gallery, which sits behind the auditorium.
✚ E4 ✉ Náměstí Jana Palacha, Staré město ☎ 2489 3111
🕐 Gallery: Tue–Sun 10–6 🚇 Staroměstská

SMETANOVA SÍŇ (SMETANA HALL)
The highly decorated 1,149-seat Smetana Hall is the grandest space in the Obecní dům (Municipal House ▶ 46). The Prague Spring music festival is heralded here every year with a rousing rendition of the symphonic poem *Má Vlast* (*My Country*).
✚ E/F4 ✉ Obecní dům, Náměstí Republiky ☎ 2200 2100
🕐 Check locally 🍴 Café and restaurant 🚇 Náměstí Republiky

STÁTNÍ OPERA PRAHA (STATE OPERA ▶ 75)

STAVOVSKÉ DIVADLO
(ESTATES THEATER ▶ 75)

VILA AMERIKA (DVOŘÁK MUSEUM)
This exquisite little villa was built for Count Michna in 1720 as a summer retreat, when this part of the New Town was still countryside. It now serves as a fascinating repository for Dvořák memorabilia (▶ 76).
✚ E6 ✉ Ke Karlovu 20, Nové město ☎ 29 82 14 🕐 Tue–Sun
10–5 🚇 I.P. Pavlova 💰 Inexpensive

A musical nation
Co Čech—to muzikant! ("All Czechs are musicians!") goes the saying, and this is certainly one of the most musical of nations. In the 18th century Bohemia supplied musicians and composers to the whole of Europe.

The beat goes on
Fueled by Radio Luxembourg and smuggled records, Czech rock 'n' roll attracted real rebels—the early fans of this "Bigbeat" sound risked jail merely for throwing an unauthorized sockhop. The Popmuseum, a new attraction on Besední street, in Malá Strana, revives the "Bigbeat" scene.

Dvořák's piano, Vila Amerika

GREEN SPACES

See Top 25 Sights for
GARDENS, VALDŠTEJNSKÝ PALÁC (➤ 34)
PETŘÍN HILL (➤ 28)

Monkish retreat

The old garden of the Franciscan monks between Václavské náměstí (Wenceslas Square) and Jungmannovo náměstí (Jungmann Square) is a welcome oasis in the heart of the city.

BAROQUE GARDENS BELOW PRAŽSKÝ HRAD

The aristocrats in their palaces in Malá Strana at the foot of Prague Castle turned their interconnecting gardens into a paradise of arbors, gazebos, fountains, and stairways. Now partially reopened after restoration, they can also be enjoyed from the castle's Ramparts Garden above.

➕ D4 ✉ Valdštejnská 10–14 and Valdštejnské náměstí 3, Malá Strana ⏰ Apr–Oct: daily 10–6 🚇 Malostranská 💷 Moderate

KAMPA ISLAND

Kampa Island was flooded regularly until the Vltava was tamed in the 1950s, discouraging building and leaving large parts of it undeveloped.

➕ D4–5 ⏰ At all times 🚋 Tram 12, 22, 23 to Hellichova or Malostranské náměstí 💷 Free

KRÁLOVSKÁ ZAHRADA (ROYAL GARDENS)

Fine old trees and formal gardens make a superb setting for several pleasure pavilions north of Prague Castle: the Baroque Riding School, the sgraffitoed Ball-Game Hall, and the beautiful Belvedere.

➕ C/D3 ✉ Královská zahrada, Hradčany ⏰ Apr–Oct: daily 10–6. 🚋 Tram 22, 23 to Královský letohrádek or Pražský hrad 💷 Free

LETENSKÉ SADY (LETNÁ PLAIN ➤ 50)

VOJANOVY SADY (VOJAN GARDENS)

A peaceful retreat hidden away amid Malá Strana.

➕ D4 ✉ U lužického semináře 17, Malá Strana ⏰ Summer: daily 8–7. Winter: daily 8–5 🚇 Malostranská 💷 Free

*Stromovka Park,
Holešovice*

Karlovo náměstí

Karlovo náměstí (Charles Square) is more of a park than a square, and is a useful resting place when pounding the sidewalks becomes too tiring in this spread-out part of town.

VRTBOVSKÁ ZAHRADA (VRTBA GARDEN)

Prague's finest individual baroque garden has a splendid staircase, sculptures, and a view over Malá Strana.

➕ D4 ✉ Karmelitská 25, Malá Strana ⏰ Apr–Oct: daily 10–6 🚋 Tram 12, 22, 23 to Malostranské náměstí 💷 Inexpensive

ZAHRADA NA VALECH (RAMPARTS GARDEN)

The gardens just to the south of Prague Castle were redesigned in the 1920s and embellished with sculptural objects, including a miniature pyramid.

➕ C–D4 ✉ Pražský hrad (Prague Castle), Hradčany ⏰ Apr–Oct: 10–6 🚇 Malostranská then uphill walk 🚋 Tram 22, 23 to Pražský hrad 💷 Free

FOR KIDS

See Top 25 Sights for
NÁRODNÍ TECHNICKÉ MUZEUM (▶ 45)
PETŘÍN HILL, WITH THE FUNICULAR, VIEWING
TOWER, HALL OF MIRRORS, OBSERVATORY
(▶ 28)

CHANGING OF THE GUARD, PRAŽSKÝ HRAD

The blue-uniformed Castle Guard is ceremonially relieved every day at noon at the western gate of Prague Castle, with extra pomp on Sundays.
🞤 C4 ⊠ Pražský hrad, Hradčany 🕒 Daily at noon 🚋 Tram 22, 23 to Pražský hrad 🎫 Free

HISTORIC TRAM RIDE

A vintage tram trundles round a circuit linking downtown, Malá Strana, and the Exhibition Grounds.

MILITARY MUSEUM, ŠVARCENBERSKÝ PALÁC (▶ 54)

ORLOJ (ASTRONOMICAL CLOCK)

Crowds gather every hour on the hour in front of the Old Town Hall to enjoy the performance put on by this fascinating clock, which not only tells the time but gives the position of the sun, moon, and much more, while the splendid painted calendar shows saints' days, the signs of the zodiac, and the labors of the months. Legend has it that Hanuš, the master technician who perfected the mechanism, was blinded by the city fathers to stop him passing his secrets on. But Hanuš persuaded an apprentice to lead him up inside the clock. He then plunged his hands into the mechanism, putting it out of action for 80 years.
🞤 E4 ⊠ Staroměstské náměstí 🕒 Performances daily on the hour 9–9 🚇 Staroměstská 🎫 Free

PUPPET THEATERS (▶ 80)

VÝSTAVIŠTĚ (EXHIBITION GROUNDS)

The extensive Exhibition Grounds in the inner suburb of Holešovice have old-fashioned rides among other attractions.
🞤 E–F2 ⊠ U Výstaviště, Holešovice ☎ 2010 3204 🕒 Tue–Fri from 2PM; Sat–Sun from 10AM (evening opening for performances) 🍴 Cafés and restaurants 🚋 Tram 5, 12, 17 to Výstaviště 🎫 Inexpensive

ZOOLOGICKÁ ZAHRADA (ZOO)

Not world-class, but useful to know about and conveniently placed opposite Troja Château (▶ 48).
🞤 D1 ⊠ U Trojského zámku 3, Troja ☎ 688 0480 🕒 May–Sep: daily 9–6. Oct–Apr: daily 9–4 🍴 Buffet 🚇 Nádraží Holešovice, then bus 112 to Zoologická zahrada 🎫 Inexpensive

Keeping 'em happy

There are enough jazz bands, sword-swallowers, and other entertainers on the streets to keep kids happily staring for hours, not to mention any number of tall towers to climb. For junior travelers who prefer a more structured experience, there are now two Old Town wax museums, both offering a line-up of Czech historical and legendary personalities. A more high-tech attraction is the multimedia St. Michael Mystery, just off Staroměstské náměstí (Old Town Square). Visitors are guided through the history and legends of Prague, helped by projected holograms, sound effects, and laser lights.

Getting around

Tram rides are a novelty to many children—and excellent for getting to know the city. Other entertaining ways of moving around include the "train" that chugs up to Prague Castle from Old Town Square and the horse-drawn carriages, also based in Old Town Square.

Communist Mementoes

Communist corruption

Despite being lowered every evening into a refrigerated chamber and receiving the attentions of the best embalmers available, the corpse of Klement Gottwald (1896–1953, Czechoslovakia's first Communist president), in the National Memorial, continued to putrefy. When platoons of Young Pioneers were brought to admire their leader, most of what they saw was not Klement, but skillfully crafted replacement parts.

Home sweet home

The housing blocks known as *Paneláks* are regarded with a mixture of affection and exasperation. Any accommodations are desirable in a city with an acute housing shortage, especially if they are supplied with hot and cold running water and central heating like most *paneláks*. The downside is the dreariness of the surroundings.

BARTOLOMĚJSKÁ POLICE STATION
The police station where Václav Havel was regularly brought in for interrogation in his dissident days has now been returned to its former owners, an order of nuns, who have leased part of it as a pension. If you book far enough ahead, you can sleep in Havel's cell.
🕂 E4/5 ⊠ Pension Unitas, Bartolomějská 9, Staré město ☎ 2421 1020 🚇 Národní třída 🚹 Accessible only to pension guests

HOLIDAY INN PRAGUE
A totally authentic example of the monumental wedding-cake architecture of the Stalinist era.
🕂 C2 ⊠ Koulova 15, Dejvice ☎ 2439 3111 🚻 Café and restaurant 🚇 Dejvická then tram 20, 25 to Podbaba 🚹 Expensive to stay

JAN PALACH'S GRAVE, OLŠANSKÉ HŘBITOVY
The grave of the self-immolating student Jan Palach (▶ 43) is in the vast cemetery at Olšany. A square in the Old Town is also named after him, and flowers are regularly placed on the spot in Wenceslas Square where he burned himself to death in 1969, in protest at the Soviet occupation.
🕂 H–J5 ⊠ Olšanské hřbitovy (Olšany cemetery), Vinohradská 🕓 Daily 8–7 🚇 Flora or Želivského 🚹 Free

MEMORIAL TO NOVEMBER 17, 1989
In an arcade on Národní, a little memorial panel of hands raised in supplication marks where 50,000 student demonstrators were attacked by riot police—an event seen as the genesis of the Velvet Revolution.
🕂 E5 ⊠ Národní 16, Nové město 🚇 Národní třída 🚹 Free

THE METRO
Prague's Metro once sported a number of fine examples of Socialist-Realist art. The most visible is the mosaic of a chisel-chinned worker and his mate at Anděl station.
🕂 D6 🕓 5AM–midnight 🚇 Anděl

NÁRODNÍ PAMÁTNÍK (NATIONAL MEMORIAL)
Built in the interwar period, this slab of a building atop the steep rise to the east of the downtown area served as a shrine to prominent Communist Party men. The memorial's future is uncertain.
🕂 G4 ⊠ U památníku, Žižkov, 🚇 Florenc then uphill walk 🚌 133, 207

PANELÁKS
All around the outskirts of Prague are the monolithic housing estates composed of high-rise blocks nicknamed *paneláks*, system-built on the Soviet model from concrete panels manufactured on site.

PRAGUE
where to...

CZECH CUISINE

Prices

Expect to pay per person for dinner, excluding drinks:

$ = Kč100–250

$$ = Kč250–700

$$$ = Above Kč700

All the restaurants listed are open daily for lunch and dinner unless otherwise stated.

Dumplings

Love them or leave them, *knedliky* (dumplings) are the inevitable accompaniment to much Czech cooking, adding further solidity to an already substantial cuisine. Every housewife has her prized recipe, using bread, flour, potatoes, or semolina, and the homemade *knedlik* may have a lightness often absent from a restaurant's offering.

FREGATA ($$)

An alternative to the Vltava (► 63) for traditional fish dishes.

✚ E6 ✉ Ladova 3 (between Trojická and Plavecká) ☎ 29 31 21 🚇 Karlovo náměstí

MALOSTRANSKÁ BESEDA ($)

Czech food in Malá Strana Square.

✚ D4 ✉ Malostranské náměstí ☎ 5753 0428 🚇 Malostranská

MYSLIVNA ($$)

Improbably located in a back street in suburban Vinohrady, The Hunter's Lodge is worth seeking out for its delicious game dishes.

✚ G5 ✉ Jagellonská 21, Vinohrady ☎ 627 0209 🚇 Jiřího z Poděbrad

NA OŘECHOVCE ($$)

Pub-restaurant with some of the city's best Czech food, deep in the garden suburb of Ořechovka (Walnut Grove).

✚ B3 ✉ Východní 7, Dejvice ☎ 312 4842 🚋 Tram 1, 2, 18 to Sibeliova

PLZEŇSKÁ RESTAURACE ($$)

In the basement of the Municipal House (► 46) is this art-nouveau designer's idea of what a Bohemian beer hall should look like.

✚ E/F4 ✉ Náměstí Republiky 5, Staré město ☎ 2200 2780 🚇 Náměstí Republiky

POD KŘÍDLEM ($$$)

Stylish surroundings and impeccable food. Also close to the National Theater.

✚ E5 ✉ Národní 10, Nové město ☎ 2491 2377 🚇 Národní třída

RESTAURACE NA POŘÍČÍ ($)

An unpretentious but well-run corner restaurant frequented mostly by locals but happy to welcome tourists. Close to Masaryk station and the Municipal House.

✚ F4 ✉ Na poříčí 20, Nové město ☎ 2481 1363 🚇 Náměstí Republiky

STARÁ RADNICE ($$)

A handy lunch-stop along the Hradčany tourist trail.

✚ C4 ✉ Loretánská 1, Hradčany ☎ 2051 1140 🚋 Tram 22, 23 to Pražský hrad or Pohořelec

U BENEDIKTA ($$)

Conventional Czech cooking with some sophistication, served in a patio behind the big Kotva department store.

✚ E4 ✉ Benediktská 11, Staré město ☎ 2482 6912 🚇 Náměstí Republiky

U ČIŽKŮ ($$)

Attractive Old Bohemian farmhouse setting with meaty specialties to match, such as platters of duck, pork, and sausage with dumplings and sauerkraut.

✚ E5 ✉ Karlovo náměstí 34, Nové město ☎ 2223 2257 🚇 Karlovo náměstí

U KALICHA ($$)

Thanks to the Good Soldier Švejk's patronage in Austro-Hungarian days, this place is popular with visitors from abroad familiar with the famous Czech antihero. Solid food among much Švejkian memorabilia.

🚏 E/F5/6 ✉ Na bojišti 12–14, Nové město ☎ 9618 9600 🚇 I.P. Pavlova

U MATOUŠE ($)

Traditional dishes plus innovative but still authentic explorations into what Czech (and Moravian) cuisine is all about. Give 24 hours notice if you want to feast on roast duckling cooked as it really should be.

🚏 D5 ✉ Preslova 17, Smíchov ☎ 5731 8864 🚇 Anděl

U MIKULÁŠE DAČICKÉHO ($$)

Set designers from the famous Barrandov film studios fitted out this Czech restaurant as a medieval banqueting hall in the 1920s. Hearty food.

🚏 D5 ✉ Viktora Huga 2, Smíchov ☎ 5732 2334 🕐 Closed Sun 🚇 Anděl

U PASTÝŘKY ($$)

The rustic log cabin with a big open fireplace at The Little Shepherdess serves up tasty Slovak meals.

🚏 F5/6 ✉ Bělehradská 15, Nusle ☎ 2256 0572 🕐 Dinner only 🚋 Tram 11, 18 to Náměstí bratří Synků

U PLEBÁNA ($$)

Any old prole can eat here now, though before 1989 this place, The Plebeian, was the preserve of Communist Party bigwigs. Now local and foreign

business folk enjoy juicy duckling and succulent mixed grills.

🚏 E4 ✉ Betlémské náměstí 10, Staré město ☎ 2222 1568 🚇 Národní třída

U SEDMI ŠVÁBŮ ($–$$)

This is the place for a rollicking medieval feast. Sit around the big hearth or at companionable benches and dine on "genuine" 15th-century dishes as minstrels play.

🚏 C4 ✉ Jánský vršek 14, Malá Strana ☎ 5753 1455 🚋 Tram 12, 22, 23 to Malostranské náměstí

U SV. VALENTINA ($)

Small and surprisingly elegant considering the prices for a good range of pork, beef, and fish dishes.

🚏 E4 ✉ Veleslavínova 5, Staré město ☎ 232 7622 🚇 Staroměstská

U ZLATÉ HRUŠKY ($$$)

The Golden Pear, in a charming rococo house in romantic Nový Svět, has an attractive outdoor section.

🚏 C4 ✉ Nový Svět 3, Hradčany ☎ 2051 5356 🚋 Tram 22, 23 to Brusnice

VLTAVA ($)

Soup, carp, and trout served close to the Vltava (from which one hopes the ingredients have not been fished).

🚏 E5 ✉ Between Jiráskův most and Palackého most, Rašínovo nábřeží, Nové město ☎ 2492 2086 🚇 Karlovo náměstí

Alive, alive o!

Cut off from the sea, Czechs have traditionally made much of freshwater fish such as trout and carp. The huge ponds constructed in the Middle Ages in which the carp in particular were bred by the thousand are still very much in use. Carp make up the traditional Christmas Eve dinner, and are bought live by sharp-eyed buyers from the equally sharp dealers who set up fish tanks in the streets and squares in the days leading up to the holiday.

INTERNATIONAL CUISINE

Beware

Since 1989, restaurants targeted at a specifically foreign clientele have multiplied in number. The temptation has been to charge international prices without providing a corresponding level of food, setting, or service. Always study your checks, and give a tip only if service has been satisfactory.

AMERICAN

BUFFALO BILL'S ($–$$)
Tacos, tortilla soup, and other Tex-Mex delicacies can be enjoyed here.
🚹 E5 ⊠ Vodičkova 9
☎ 2494 8624 🚇 Můstek

RED HOT & BLUES ($–$$)
Cajun chicken, creole gumbo, and other southern specialties, plus live jazz and blues in the evenings.
🚹 E4 ⊠ Jakubská 12, Staré město ☎ 231 4639
🚇 Náměstí Republiky

ASIAN

MAILSI ($–$$)
Spicy vegetarian, chicken, and lamb dishes are favorites at this friendly neighborhood Pakistani restaurant.
🚹 G4 ⊠ Lipanská 1, Žižkov
☎ 9005 9706 🚊 Tram 5, 9, 26 to Lipanská

PRAHA TAMURA ($$$)
Unthinkable a few years ago—an excellent Japanese restaurant in the heart of Prague's Old Town.
🚹 E4 ⊠ Havelská 6, Staré město ☎ 2423 2056
🚇 Můstek

RASOI ($$)
A popular restaurant serving tandoori and curries in the downstairs restaurant and lighter food in the Bombay Café.
🚹 E4 ⊠ Dlouhá 13, Staré město ☎ 232 8400
🚇 Staroměstská

SATÉ ($)
Before 1989, no Czech porker expected to end up as satay on a skewer, but Indonesian eating has now colonized this square in upper Hradčany.
🚹 C4 ⊠ Pohořelec 152/3, Hradčany ☎ 2051 4552
🚊 Tram 22, 23 to Pohořelec

CONTINENTAL

CERBERUS ($$)
Attractive setting for Czech and continental cooking. In the New Town, not far from the Obecní dům (Municipal House ➤ 46).
🚹 F4 ⊠ Soukenická 19, Nové město ☎ 2481 4118
🚇 Closed Sun 🚇 Náměstí Republiky

DAVID ($$$)
An intimate setting and faultless food, including melt-in-the-mouth lamb, a house specialty.
🚹 D4 ⊠ Tržiště 21, Malá Strana ☎ 5753 3109
🚊 Tram 22, 23 to Malostranské náměstí

KAMPA PARK ($$–$$$)
Stylish food in a pretty pink house on Kampa Island.
🚹 D4 ⊠ Na Kampě 8b, Malá Strana ☎ 5753 2685
🚇 Malostranská 🚊 Tram 12, 22, 23 to Malostranské náměstí

KLÁŠTERNÍ VINÁRNA ($$)
Steaks are excellent in The Monastery wine restaurant.
🚹 E5 ⊠ Národní 8, Nové město ☎ 29 05 96
🚇 Národní třída

LOBKOVICKÁ VINÁRNA ($$$)

The cooking is imaginative in this wine restaurant run by the aristocratic Lobkovics. Wines are from the family estate at Mělník.

✚ C4 ⊠ Vlašská 17, Malá Strana ☎ 53 01 85
🚊 Tram 12, 22, 23 to Malostranské náměstí

SVATÁ KLÁRA ($$$)

Dine discreetly on game, duck and other elegant fare in the aristocratic Trojský zámek.

✚ D1 ⊠ U trojského zámku 9 ☎ 688 0405 🕐 Dinner only; reservations essential
🚊 Nádraží Holešovice then bus 112 to Zoologická zahrada

U MODRÉ KACHNIČKY ($$$)

The Blue Duckling was an instant success when it opened in 1993. First-rate game is served in its intimate, antiques-furnished rooms.

✚ D4 ⊠ Nebovidská 6, Malá Strana ☎ 5732 0308
🚊 Tram 12, 22, 23 to Hellichova

U MODRÉ RŮŽE ($$$)

The Blue Rose, in an atmospheric Old Town basement, serves notable fish and game.

✚ E4 ⊠ Rytířská 16, Staré město ☎ 2422 5873
🚊 Můstek

VAS-Y VAS-Y ($$)

French-inspired dishes at reasonable prices, served in a tiny bar-dining room near the Globe bookstore.

✚ E5 ⊠ Pštrossova 8, Nové město ☎ 29 13 52 🕐 Closed Sun 🚊 Národní třída or Karlovo náměstí

V ZATIŠÍ ($$$)

All-round excellence and sophistication just off the Royal Way. This fine restaurant (whose name means "still life" or "seclusion") opened not long after the Velvet Revolution and is now a Prague institution.

✚ E4 ⊠ Liliová 1, Staré město ☎ 2222 1155 🚊 Staroměstská

FRENCH

LA PROVENCE ($$$)

A range of French specialties, from cassoulet to coq au vin.

✚ E4 ⊠ Štupartská 9, Staré město ☎ 9005 4510
🚊 Náměstí Republiky

U MALÍŘŮ ($$$)

The French food served in The Painter is sublime. It's in an ancient house in the middle of Malá Strana.

✚ D4 ⊠ Maltézské náměstí 11, Malá Strana ☎ 5753 0318
🚊 Tram 12, 22, 23 to Hellichova

GREEK

FAROS ($$)

Moussaka and other Greek specialties.

✚ C4 ⊠ Šporkova 5, Malá Strana ☎ 5753 3964
🚊 Tram 22, 23 to Malostranské náměstí

GRILLS

OPERA GRILL ($$$)

Fabulous food in an intimate setting that oozes elegance.

✚ E4 ⊠ Karoliny Světlé 35, Staré město ☎ 26 55 08
🚊 Národní třída

Local fast food

Western fast food is now available in many places, but better by far (and much cheaper) for a quick snack are the local *obložené chlebíčky* (open-faced sandwiches). Each of these is like a miniature meal, perhaps consisting of a sliver or two of ham or salami and a slice of hard-boiled egg, the whole garnished with mayonnaise and topped with pieces of pickle and red pepper.

Czech wines and liquor

Although little known abroad, Czech wines are surprisingly good, especially both reds and whites from Moravia, and make an interesting souvenir. Liquor is cheap and often excellent. Slivovice (plum brandy) is well known, a supposed cure for all ills, while Becherovka, prepared in Carlsbad to a secret recipe, has a unique and pungent flavor.

ROTISSERIE ($$)
A long-established grill that has maintained its standards in the face of much competition.
✚ E5 ✉ Mikulandská 6, Nové město ☎ 2491 4557 Ⓜ Národní třída

ITALIAN

BELLA NAPOLI ($–$$)
Not just Neapolitan food but a range of other Italian delights, only a short step from Wenceslas Square.
✚ E5 ✉ V jámě 8, Nové město ☎ 2223 2933 Ⓜ Muzeum

DON GIOVANNI ($$–$$$)
Italian panache with a view over the River Vltava.
✚ E4 ✉ Karoliny Světlé 34, Staré město ☎ 2222 2060 Ⓜ Staroměstská

IL RITROVO ($–$$)
An amiable Florentine restaurant near Wenceslas Square, designed to make Italian expats feel *a casa*.
✚ F5/6 ✉ Lublaňská 11, Vinohrady ☎ 2426 1475 Ⓜ I.P. Pavlova

OSTROFF ($$$)
Sounds Russian, tastes like Italian. A very trendy restaurant and bar on Shooters' Island.
✚ D5 ✉ Střelecký ostrov 336 ☎ 2491 9235 🚋 Tram 6, 9, 18, 22, 23 to Národní divadlo, then cross Most Legii (Legions' Bridge) to Střelecký ostrov (Shooters' Island)

MIDDLE EASTERN

ADONIS ($)
A popular lunch spot offering a whole range of Middle Eastern delicacies.
✚ E5 ✉ Jungmannova 21, Nové město ☎ 2494 8452 Ⓜ Můstek or Národní třída

FAKHRELDINE ($$$)
A branch of this internationally famous restaurant group. Serves Lebanese food.
✚ E5 ✉ Štěpánská 32, Nové město ☎ 2223 2617 Ⓜ Muzeum

SEAFOOD

NA RYBÁRNĚ ($$)
Fishy delights in a restaurant supposedly once frequented by President Havel and cronies.
✚ E5/6 ✉ Gorazdova 17, Nové město ☎ 2491 8885 Ⓜ Karlovo náměstí

REYKJAVÍK ($$)
A welcome stop along the tourist trail between Old Town Square and Charles Bridge, this Icelandic establishment serves fresh fish flown in from the cold North Atlantic.
✚ E4 ✉ Karlova 20, Staré město ☎ 2222 1218 Ⓜ Staroměstská

RYBÍ TRH ($$$)
One of the widest selections of seafood in the city, in the low-key dining room or vaulted wine cellar.
✚ E4 ✉ Týn 5 (between Týnská and Štupartská), Staré město ☎ 2489 5447 Ⓜ Náměstí Republiky

VEGETARIAN & SCENIC RESTAURANTS

VEGETARIAN

COUNTRY LIFE ($)
Healthful eating and food shopping in the heart of the Old Town.
➕ E4 ✉ Melantrichova 15, Staré město ☎ 2421 3366 🚇 Můstek

GOVINDA VEGETARIAN CLUB ($)
As much wholefood as you can digest at this Hare Krishna restaurant/bakery/tea room, in a convenient location not far from the art-nouveau Obecní dům (Municipal House ➤ 46).
➕ F4 ✉ Soukenicka 27, Nové město ☎ 2481 6016 🚇 Náměstí Republiky

LOTOS ($$)
Refined meat-free dining for everyone from strict vegans to those who merely seek a change from the pork-heavy Czech diet.
➕ E4 ✉ Platnéřská 13, Staré město ☎ 232 2390 🚇 Staroměstská

RADOST CAFÉ FX ($)
Trendy café; *très chic.*
➕ F6 ✉ Bělehradská 120, Vinohrady ☎ 2425 4776 🚇 I.P. Pavlova

RESTAURANTS WITH A VIEW OR TERRACE

HANAVSKÝ PAVILON ($$$)
The delightful little art-nouveau Hanava Pavilion, perched high above the River Vltava, serves mostly foreign guests. It offers continental cuisine, as well as Bohemian game and poultry dishes.
➕ D3 ✉ Letenské sady 173, Letná ☎ 3332 3641 🚋 Tram 18 to Chotkovy sady

NEBOZÍZEK ($$)
The Little Auger looks the other way from the Parnas, from the slopes of Petřín Hill toward the center. Continental food. Reached by funicular.
➕ C5 ✉ Petřínské sady 411, Malá Strana ☎ 53 79 05 🚟 Funicular

PARNAS ($$$)
For a special night out. Sumptuous setting and sophisticated continental cuisine combined with an unbeatable view of the Vltava and Prague Castle. Reserve a window table.
➕ D5 ✉ Smetanovo nábřeží 2, Staré město ☎ 2421 8493 🚇 Národní třída

RESTAURACE NA VYŠEHRADĚ ($)
With its terrace and straightforward Czech cooking, this is a good place to cool off after visiting Prague's second citadel.
➕ E7 ✉ Štulcova 2, Vyšehrad ☎ 2423 9298 🚇 Vyšehrad

U KRISTIANA ($$)
Unmemorable food but a prospect to die for. Christian's is aboard a barge anchored below the Smetana Embankment. Order anything and savor the view across the Vltava to Charles Bridge, Malá Strana, and the castle.
➕ D4 ✉ Smetanovo nábřeží, Staré město ☎ 9000 0601 🚋 Tram 17, 18 to Karlovy lázně or 6, 9, 21, 22 to Národní divadlo

Veggie revolution

Before 1989, vegetarians venturing to Prague were liable to be served endless omelets, perhaps with extra dumplings. Czechs still like their rich and hearty meat-based dishes, but waiters and others are no longer fazed when a foreigner expresses an interest in something else.

Kosher food

Reliable kosher food can be had at Kosher Restaurant Shalom ($–$$), in the former meeting room of the Jewish Town Hall (➕ E4 ✉ Maislova 18, Staré město ☎ 2481 0929 🚇 Staroměstská).

Pubs

Czech beer

Lager beer was virtually invented in Bohemia, when the citizens of Plzeň (Pilsen) got together to form the Burghers' Brewery in 1842 and began producing the light and tasty liquid that has spawned endless imitation "pils" ever since but which has never been surpassed. But other Czech beers are just as good, better from the barrel than the bottle. Try Prague's own Staropramen or Braník, or the milder Budvar from České Budějovice (Budweis) in southern Bohemia.

BRANICKÁ FORMANKA

The suburban Braník brewery is one of four major breweries in Prague. This pub is its downtown outlet.
✚ E5 ✉ Vodičkova 26, Nové město ⓠ Můstek

ČERNÝ OREL

An enclosed courtyard and rustic interior lend this inn the feeling of being miles removed from the bustling city streets.
✚ D4 ✉ U Lužického semináře 40, Malá Strana ☎ 5753 1738 ⓠ Malostranská

JAMES JOYCE

Guinness and other Irish beers—should you tire of the wonders of Czech beer.
✚ E4 ✉ Liliová 10, Staré město ☎ 2424 8793 ⓠ Staroměstská

NOVOMĚSTSKÝ PIVOVAR

The New Town Brewery is one of the city's small contingent of microbrewery-restaurants. Prices are more reasonable than at tourist-deluged U Fleků.
✚ E5 ✉ Vodičkova 20, Nové město ☎ 2223 1662 ⓠ Můstek

U FLEKŮ

Every visitor should sip the dark and tasty beer that has been brewed and served on these raucous premises for 200 years. There's also a big beer garden.
✚ E5 ✉ Křemencova 11, Nové město ☎ 2491 5118 ⓠ Karlovo náměstí or Národní třída

U KOCOURA

The famous old Tomcat is a welcome sight on the hard trek up from Malá Strana to Prague Castle.
✚ D4 ✉ Nerudova 2, Malá Strana ⓠ Tram 12, 22, 23 to Malostranské náměstí

U MEDVÍDKŮ

Budvar, from the town of České Budějovice in southern Bohemia, is probably the best-known Bohemian beer apart from Pilsener. Try it here on tap—out in the garden in summer.
✚ E4 ✉ Na Perštýně 7, Staré město ⓠ Národní třída

U SVATÉHO TOMÁŠE

The monks no longer brew their own here, but medieval St. Thomas's is a popular stop for tour groups. Folk-music performances.
✚ D4 ✉ Letenská 12, Malá Strana ⓠ Malostranská

U VEJVODŮ

Remodeled, enlarged, and cleaned up, this ancient pub appeals to visitors and locals alike.
✚ E4 ✉ Jilská 4, Staré město ☎ 2421 9205 ⓠ Národní třída

U ZLATÉHO TYGRA

Perfect Pilsener, drawn straight from the pub's 13th-century cellars, has made The Golden Tiger a favorite with serious local drinkers.
✚ E4 ✉ Husova 17, Staré město ☎ 2222 1111 ⓠ Staroměstská

BARS AND CAFÉS

ARCHA
This café, next to the popular theater/concert hall of the same name, attracts a youthful, intellectual set.
✚ F4 ✉ Na poříčí 26, north Nové město ☎ 232 4149 Ⓜ Náměstí Republiky

CAFÉ LOUVRE
A famous establishment now under its original name, the Louvre is decorated in rococo style and offers everything from breakfast to billiards.
✚ E5 ✉ Národní 20, Nové město ☎ 29 72 23 Ⓜ Národní třída

CAFÉ MILENA
Another elegant café in Old Town Square.
✚ E4 ✉ Staroměstské náměstí 22, Staré město ☎ 2163 2602 Ⓜ Staroměstská

CAFÉ SAVOY
Refined early 20th-century café at the Malá Strana end of the Legions' Bridge (Most Legií).
✚ D5 ✉ Vítězná 5, Malá Strana 🚋 Tram 6, 9, 22, 23 to Újezd

CAFFÉ DANTE
Streamlined Italian café opposite the modern art collections of the Trades Fair Palace.
✚ F3 ✉ Dukelských hrdinů 16, Holešovice ☎ 87 01 93 🚋 Tram 5, 12, 17 to Veletržni

DOBRÁ ČAJOVNA
Hidden in a courtyard just yards from the jostling crowds of Wenceslas Square is the aromatic Good Tea Room, where you can taste a huge variety of teas in a mellow, smoke-free atmosphere.
✚ E5 ✉ Václavské náměstí 14, Nové město ☎ 2423 1480 Ⓜ Můstek

DOLCE VITA
Authentic espresso close to Old Town Square.
✚ E4 ✉ Široká 15, Staré město ☎ 232 9192 Ⓜ Staroměstská

EVROPA
It takes arrogance for a café to charge an entrance fee, as does the art-nouveau café of the Evropa Hotel. Still, the place is not to be missed.
✚ E5 ✉ Václavské náměstí 25, Nové město ☎ 2422 8117 Ⓜ Můstek

SLAVIA
This classic Central European café, with its view over the Vltava, is open again after a long and controversial closure.
✚ D5 ✉ Smetanovo nábřeží 2, Staré město ☎ 2422 0957 Ⓜ Národní třída

VELRYBA
The Whale opens wide its jaws to accommodate its trendy clientele.
✚ E5 ✉ Opatovická 24, Nové město ☎ 2491 2484 Ⓜ Národní třída

Turkish coffee

Espresso, cappuccino, and most other coffees can now be found in Prague, but don't be surprised if you get served a traditional *"turecká káva."* This is Turkish coffee, fine when you're accustomed to it and know when to stop swallowing—that is before you disturb the deposit of coffee grounds at the bottom of the cup.

BOOKS & ANTIQUES

Bargains... perhaps

Czechs are great readers, and until recently new and secondhand books were very inexpensive, many of them in languages other than Czech. Prices have risen considerably since 1989, but there are still many bargains. That said, prices for antique books are now well in line with those on the international market.

NEW BOOKS

ANAGRAM
Fiction, philosophy, religion, and history in English are the specialties of this store in the bustling Týn Courtyard.
E4 ⌧ Týn 4 (between Týnská and Štupartská), Staré město ☎ 2489 5737
Ⓜ Náměstí Republiky

BIG BEN
Guidebooks and Czech literature in translation are in good supply at this small store.
E4 ⌧ Malá Štupartská 5, Staré město ☎ 2482 6565
Ⓜ Náměstí Republiky

FRANZ KAFKA
Stocks an excellent range of both new and secondhand books, mostly in German.
D4 ⌧ U lužického semináře 19, Malá Strana ☎ 53 15 52
Ⓜ Malostranská

THE GLOBE BOOKSTORE AND COFFEEHOUSE
A congenial home-away-from-home for Americans and anyone hungry for literature in English, as well as bagels and American-style coffee.
E5 ⌧ Pštrossova 6, Nové město ☎ 2491 7230
Ⓜ Národní třída or Karlovo náměstí

KANZELSBERGER
A good selection of new titles, including children's stories and books on Prague and the Czech Republic, many in languages other than Czech.

E5 ⌧ Václavské náměstí (Wenceslas Square) 42, Nové město ☎ 2421 7335
Ⓜ Můstek

KIWI
Don't be put off by the travel agency on the first floor; the store in the basement has one of the best selections of maps and guides in Prague.
E5 ⌧ Jungmannova 23, Nové město ☎ 2494 8455
Ⓜ Národní třída

KNIHKUPECTVÍ U ČERNÉ MATKY BOŽÍ
A large, well-stocked bookstore that carries a good selection of coffee-table books in English. Unmissable location in the Cubist House at the Black Madonna (► 56).
E4 ⌧ Celetná 34, Staré město ☎ 2421 1275
Ⓜ Náměstí Republiky

ANTIQUARIAN BOOKSTORES

ANTIKVARIÁT EVA KOZÁKOVÁ
Old photographs, prints, and postcards, plus innumerable old books, mostly Czech.
E5 ⌧ Myslikova 10, Nové město ☎ 29 44 02
Ⓜ Karlovo náměstí

ANTIKVARIÁT GALERIE MŮSTEK
Printed treasures of all kinds can be found in this spacious Old Town basement. Many engravings, maps, and even paintings.
E4 ⌧ 28 října 13, Staré město ☎ 2422 8655
Ⓜ Můstek

ANTIKVARIÁT KAREL KŘENEK

Refined establishment near the start of the Royal Way, with an excellent range of prints and watercolors as well as fine old books.

✚ E4 ✉ Celetná 31, Staré město ☎ 231 4734 🚇 Náměstí Republiky

ANTIKVARIÁT U KARLOVA MOSTU

Fine old books and printed memorabilia of all kinds. Not particularly inexpensive.

✚ E4 ✉ Karlova 2, Staré město ☎ 2222 0286 🚇 Staroměstská

EX LIBRIS

Intriguing secondhand books of Czech art and photography, plus many art books in German and English.

✚ E4-5 ✉ Konviktská 6, Staré město ☎ 2423 5451 🚇 Národní třída

ANTIQUES

DOROTHEUM

This branch of the long-established Vienna auction-house has a fine range of antiques of all kinds. No bargains, but no rip-offs either.

✚ E4 ✉ Ovocný trh 2, Staré město ☎ 2422 2001 🚇 Můstek or Náměstí Republiky

NA STARÉ POŠTĚ

The specialties here are 19th- and 20th-century Czech paintings, as well as old dolls and puppets. A few pieces of Rosenthal and Pirkenhammer porcelain and such oddities as walking sticks

add to the mix.

✚ D5 ✉ Maltézské náměstí 8, Malá Strana ☎ 5753 0317 🚋 Tram 12, 22, 23 to Hellichova

NOSTALGIE ANTIQUE

Old clothes and jewelry are the specialties at this engrossing little store.

✚ C4 ✉ Jánský vršek 8, Malá Strana ☎ 5753 0049 🚋 Tram 12, 22, 23 to Malostranské náměstí

PRAŽSKÉ STAROŽITNOSTI

"Prague Antiques" sells jewelry, porcelain, and paintings galore.

✚ E5 ✉ Mikulandská 8, Nové město ☎ 29 41 70 🚇 Národní třída

VLADIMÍR ANDRLE

This antiques store, in Wenceslas Square, is a handy starting point during your hunt for collectables.

✚ E5 ✉ Václavské náměstí 17, Nové město ☎ 2400 9166 🚇 Můstek

ZLATÁ KORUNA

Antique coins, medals, and paper money.

✚ E4 ✉ Pařížská 8, Staré město ☎ 231 9689 🚇 Staroměstská

ZLATNICTVÍ VOMÁČKA

Antique and secondhand jewelry, porcelain, and diverse knick-knacks.

✚ E4 ✉ Náprstkova 9, Staré město ☎ 2222 2017 🚇 Národní třída

Wenceslas Hollar

One of the first artists to make accurate drawings of the English landscape was Wenceslas Hollar. Born in 1607 in Bohemia, Václav (to give him his Czech name) sought refuge abroad following the Protestant defeat at the Battle of the White Mountain, and was employed as a draftsman by the Earl of Arundel. A trawl through Prague's antiquarian bookstores might turn up a Hollar original, such as his wonderfully detailed 1636 panorama of the city, but there are plenty of alternatives by other artists—drawings, engravings, and maps—at affordable prices.

GIFTS, SOUVENIRS & MUSIC

Kafka at home

One of the many places lived in by novelist Franz Kafka was the house on Celetná Street adjoining Kostel Panny Marie Před Týnem (Týn Church). In the bedroom in which Kafka slept and dreamed as a child, a blank window faces down the south aisle of the church's nave.

Sgraffito

The Švarcenberský palác (Schwarzenberg Palace) on Hradčanské náměstí is probably Prague's most splendidly sgraffitoed building. Sgraffito work involves picking out patterns in two shades of plasterwork either to accentuate the architectural character of the building, or to cover the facade with lively pictures, as in Martinický palác (Martinic Palace) and Hradčany Square.

TOYS, PUPPETS & SOUVENIRS

ČESKÁ LIDOVÁ ŘEMESLA

Folksy artifacts include Christmas crèches as well as willow whips with which to harass village maidens at Eastertime.
✚ E4 ✉ Jilská 22, Staré město ☎ 2222 0433 🚇 Staroměstská

DIVADELNÍ KNIHKUPECTVÍ A LOUTKY

Looking for a puppet as a souvenir? The Theater Bookstore and Marionettes sells hand-made marionettes of superior quality to those available on the street at correspondingly higher prices. Worth visiting if only to study the several kinds of Devil that play such a prominent part in Czech puppetry.
✚ E4 ✉ Celetná 17, Staré město 🚇 Náměstí Republiky

EXPOZICE FRANZE KAFKY

Prague's most famous writer must have spun around in his grave many times at the souvenir industry which has impressed his haggard features on countless T-shirts. This has the least tacky selection of *kafkeriana* in the city.
✚ E4 ✉ Corner of Maislova and Kaprova, Staré město 🚇 Staroměstská

IVRE

Lots of locally made soft toys and hand puppets.
✚ E4 ✉ Jakubská 3, Staré město 🚇 Náměstí Republiky

KID-TRNKA

Sensible and imaginative wooden toys.
✚ E5 ✉ Ostrovní 21, Nové město ☎ 26 67 53 🚇 Národní třída.

KROKODIL

New and secondhand trains galore, including rarities dating from the Communist era.
✚ D5 ✉ Bartolomějská 3, Staré město 🚇 Národní třída

LISKA

Central Europeans still wear their fur hats and coats without shame, purchased from elegant outlets such as this one near Old Town Square. If you're on a budget, look instead for fox-fur hats sold at bargain prices in the Havelská market.
✚ E4 ✉ Železná 1, Staré město 🚇 Staroměstská

MUSEUM SHOP

Unusually tasteful and original souvenirs based on the treasures of the many Prague museums, plus foreign art books not available elsewhere in Prague. An example to other souvenir stores worldwide; where else, for example, could you buy a china mug with elegant sgraffito patterning?
✚ D4 ✉ Jiřská 6, Hradčany ☎ 2437 3264 🚋 Tram 22, 23 to Pražský hrad

OBCHOD S LOUTKAMI

Another place to find a plethora of puppetry.
✚ C4 ✉ Nerudova 47, Malá Strana 🚋 Tram 12, 22, 23 to Malostranské náměstí

ARTS & CRAFTS

CASHPI
Designer glassware, a Czech specialty.
🔢 E4 ✉ Celetná 19, Staré město 🚇 Náměstí Republiky

CRYSTAL
Wonderfully decorated glass from Nový Bor in northern Bohemia.
🔢 E4 ✉ Karlova 21, 24, Staré město ☎ 25 46 25 🚇 Staroměstská

GALERIE PEITHNER-LICHTENFELS
Modern Czech and Austrian art, including works from the period between the wars.
🔢 E4 ✉ Michalská 12, Staré město ☎ 2422 7680 🚇 Můstek

GALERIE PYRAMIDA
Not all Czech glass is for serving wine. This spacious store displays art glass from some of the best Czech designers. Good-quality small bronzes and other objets d'art are also sold.
🔢 E5 ✉ Národní 11, Nové město ☎ 2421 3117 🚇 Národní třída

GRANÁT
Bohemian garnets are world-famous; this store has the most varied selection.
🔢 E4 ✉ Dlouhá 30, Staré město ☎ 231 5612 🚇 Náměstí Republiky

IVANA FOLLOVÁ ART AND FASHION
A large store in the Týn courtyard offering high quality, locally made silk dresses and scarves, jewelry and ceramics.
🔢 E4 ✉ Týn 1 (between Týnská and Štupartská), Staré město ☎ 2489 5460 🚇 Náměstí Republiky

MOSER
The outlet for the fine crystal and porcelain made in Carlsbad (Karlovy Vary), plus porcelain from Meissen and Herend.
🔢 E4 ✉ Na příkopě 12, Staré město ☎ 2421 1293 🚇 Můstek or Náměstí Republiky

SKLO BOHEMIA
Bohemian glassware from Světlá nad Sázavou.
🔢 E4 ✉ Na příkopě 17 ☎ 2421 0574 🚇 Můstek or Náměstí Republiky

MUSIC

AGHARTA
Jazz, jazz, and more jazz on sale at this nightspot.
🔢 F5 ✉ Krakovská 5, Nové město 🕐 Evenings only 🚇 Muzeum

BONTONLAND KORUNA
Reputedly the biggest music store in Central Europe, although better for pop and rock than classical music. In the labyrinthine basement of the Koruna Palace at the corner of Wenceslas Square and Na příkopě.
🔢 E4 ✉ Václavské náměstí 1, Nové město ☎ 2447 3080 🚇 Můstek

MUSICA BONA
A good selection of Czech classical music from the Middle Ages up to today.
🔢 E4 ✉ Jakubská 2, Staré město ☎ 232 0265 🚇 Náměstí Republiky

Musical miscellany

In addition to excellent discs of music by the classical composers most closely associated with the city (Mozart, Dvořák, Smetana...), Prague stores stock strongly flavored and highly individual pop music (Šum Svistu, or Laura and her Tigers, Psi vojáci...). Even more distinctive are the brass bands—the best you've ever heard—pumping out Czech (yes, Czech) old-time favorites such as "Roll Out the Barrel" ("Škoda lásky").

DEPARTMENT STORES, MARKETS & FOOD

Red Army surplus

After 1989, the Warsaw Pact crumbled and the Red Army began its long retreat back to Moscow, shedding its surplus equipment as it went. Many Czech farmers now carry a Kalashnikov rifle rather than a humble shotgun, while visitors may still find themselves tempted by the trim greatcoats or the improbably high-peaked officers' caps that are on sale wherever tourists congregate.

DEPARTMENT STORES

BÍLÁ LABUŤ

The White Swan is a long-established department store on an unfashionable but interesting shopping street just east of the Old Town. A branch is now open on Wenceslas Square opposite the National Museum.

✚ F4 ✉ Na Poříčí 23, north Nové město 🚇 Náměstí Republiky

KOTVA

The Anchor was completed in 1975 and for a while was the city's foremost shopping site, though the range of goods would have seemed basic to Western consumers. Nowadays, though the anodized aluminum and tinted glass exterior remains as intimidating as ever, it is full of fine things from all over the world.

✚ E4 ✉ Náměstí Republiky 8, Staré město 🚇 Náměstí Republiky

KRONE

A German equivalent of Tesco, on Wenceslas Square.

✚ E4 ✉ Václavské náměstí 21 🚇 Můstek

TESCO

Rival to Kotva, and once bearing the impeccably proletarian name of "Máj" (May), this department store is now in British hands. A ride up the escalator gives a good view of downtown.

✚ E5 ✉ Národní 26, Nové město 🚇 Národní třída

MARKETS

HAVELSKÁ/ V KOTCÍCH

Atmospheric market for fruits, vegetables, and souvenirs.

✚ E4 ✉ Staré město 🕐 Daily 🚇 Můstek

HOLEŠOVICKÁ TRŽNICE

Comprehensive market on the far side of the Vltava, north of Old Town.

✚ G3 ✉ Bubenské nábřeží, Holešovice 🕐 Daily 🚇 Vltavská

PRAŽSKÁ BURZA

Cheap clothes, motor parts, and an abundance of things you won't want—a fascinating spectacle.

✚ F2 ✉ Výstaviště (Exhibition Grounds), Holešovice 🕐 Sat–Sun 10–2 🚊 Tram 5, 12, 17 to Výstaviště

FOOD SHOPS

COUNTRY LIFE

Healthy natural foods— elsewhere hard to find in this calorie-addicted city.

✚ E4 ✉ Melantrichova 15, Staré město 🚇 Můstek

FRUITS DE FRANCE

French Fruits changed the face of food shopping in Prague not long after the Velvet Revolution, and is still the place for classy imported foods.

✚ E4 ✉ Jindřišská 9, Nové město 🚇 Můstek

UZENINY

Every kind of Central European sausage.

✚ E5 ✉ Václavské náměstí 34 🚇 Můstek

OPERA & CHURCH CONCERTS

OPERA

HUDEBNÍ DIVADLO V KARLÍNĚ (KARLÍN MUSICAL THEATER)

Operettas and musicals are the undemanding fare in this theater in Karlín.

🚼 F4 ✉ Křižíkova 10, Karlín ☎ 2186 8149
🚇 Florenc

NÁRODNÍ DIVADLO (NATIONAL THEATER)

Operas from both the Czech and international repertoire are performed in a sumptuous setting in the National Theater (➤ 36).

STÁTNÍ OPERA PRAHA (STATE OPERA)

Opened in 1887 as the Deutsches Theater (German Theater), this neo-Renaissance building became the Smetanovo divadlo (Smetana Theater) after World War II. It's now the State Opera, with performances from the international repertoire and classical ballet.

🚼 F5 ✉ Wilsonova 4, Nové město ☎ 26 53 53
🚇 Muzeum

STAVOVSKÉ DIVADLO (ESTATES THEATER)

The venue that saw the premiere of Mozart's *Don Giovanni* in 1787 is a marvel of pristine neoclassical glory. Regular performances of Wolfgang's greatest hits can be enjoyed here.

🚼 E4 ✉ Ovocný trh, Staré město ☎ 2490 1448
🚇 Můstek

CONCERTS IN CHURCHES

ANEŽSKÝ KLÁŠTER (ST. AGNES'S CONVENT)

Chamber music in one of the convent's two churches (➤ 41).

BAZILIKA SV. JIŘÍ (ST. GEORGE'S BASILICA)

The castle's austere Romanesque church is now used for chamber concerts (➤ 31).

CHRÁM SV. MIKULÁŠE (ST. NICHOLAS'S CHURCH), MALÁ STRANA

The organ that Mozart played in Prague's greatest baroque church still accompanies choral concerts (➤ 33).

KOSTEL SV. JAKUBA (ST. JAMES'S CHURCH)

The admirable acoustics in this Old Town church augment the concerts of sacred music held here (➤ 55).

KOSTEL SV. MIKULÁŠE, STARÉ MĚSTO (ST. NICHOLAS'S CHURCH, OLD TOWN)

The other Church of St. Nicholas is less sumptuous than the one in Malá Strana but an equally fine choice for organ and vocal recitals (➤ 55).

Mozart in Prague

"My Praguers understand me," declared Mozart, who was far better received here than in Vienna. Both *Figaro* and *Don Giovanni* were hits in Prague, and after his pauper's death in Vienna, it was Prague that honored him with a great funeral mass in Malá Strana's St. Nicholas's Church, attended by a crowd of 4,000 mourners.

CONCERTS IN OTHER VENUES

Josef Kajetán Tyl

The Stavovské divadlo (Estates Theater ► 75) reverted to its original name in 1991. For many years it was called the Tyl Theater; almost unknown abroad, the 19th-century playwright Josef Kajetán Tyl is dear to Czech hearts for his comedy *Fidlovačka*, which contains the song *"Kde domov můj?"* ("Where is my home?"), a plaintive call that later was adopted as the Czechoslovak national anthem.

BERTRAMKA (MOZART MUSEUM)

Mozart's Prague patrons, the Dušeks, once lived here and it is where the composer finished *Don Giovanni*. The museum (► 53) stages regular concerts .

✚ D4 ✉ Jiřská 3, Hradčany

CLAM-GALLASŮV PALÁC (CLAM-GALLAS PALACE)

Chamber concerts in a gargantuan Old Town mansion otherwise rarely open to the public.

✚ E4 ✉ Husova 20, Staré město ⓖ Staroměstská

DŮM U KAMMENÉHO ZVONU (HOUSE AT THE STONE BELL)

Contemporary classical pieces spark a traditional repertoire performed in a Gothic mansion on Old Town Square.

✚ E4 ✉ Staroměstské náměstí 13, Staré město ☎ 2482 7526 ⓖ Staroměstská

KLEMENTINUM

This vast complex hosts chamber concerts in its Hall of Mirrors (Zrcadlová síň).

✚ E4 ✉ Entrances at Karlova 1, Mariánské náměstí, and Křižovnické náměstí, Staré město ⓖ Staroměstská

LICHTENŠTEJNSKÝ PALÁC (LIECHTENSTEIN PALACE)

Palatial setting for symphonic and other performances.

✚ D4 ✉ Malostranské náměstí 13, Malá Strana ☎ 53 09 43 ⓖ Tram 12, 22, 23 to Malostranské náměstí

LOBKOVICKÝ PALÁC (LOBKOVIC PALACE)

Chamber concerts in the banqueting hall of a palace near the castle precinct.

✚ D4 ✉ Jiřská 3, Hradčany ☎ 53 73 06 ⓖ Malostranská then uphill walk ⓖ Tram 22, 23 to Pražský hrad

RUDOLFINUM

The Dvořák Hall of this splendid neo-Renaissance hall on the Vltava is the home of the Czech Philharmonic Orchestra. The Little (or Suk) Hall is used for chamber concerts.

✚ E4 ✉ Alšovo nábřeži 12, Staré město ☎ 2489 3352 ⓖ Staroměstská

SMETANOVA SÍŇ (SMETANA HALL)

Part of the sumptuously decorated Municipal House, and home of the Prague Symphony Orchestra (► 57).

TROJSKÝ ZÁMEK (TROJA CHÂTEAU)

The magnificence of Count Šternberg's out-of-town palace almost overwhelms the music (► 48).

VALDŠTEJNSKÝ PALÁC (WALLENSTEIN PALACE)

Wonderful summer evening concerts in the baroque gardens (► 34).

VILA AMERIKA

Count Michna's jolly little 18th-century summer palace, home of the Dvořák Museum, stages tributes to the composer's life and work (► 57).

POP & ROCK

CLUB MECCA
Local DJs and guests from Europe's leading dance palaces spin records in this club out in a gentrifying industrial district. The adjacent restaurant attracts a similarly style-conscious crowd.

➕ G2 ✉ U Průhonu 3, Holešovice ☎ 8387 1520
Ⓜ Vltavská, then tram 1, 3, 14, 25 to Dělnická

LÁVKA
Come here for dancing to recorded music on the riverside close to Prague's most celebrated bridge, Karlův most (Charles Bridge).

➕ D4 ✉ Novotného lávka 1, Staré město ☎ 2222 2156
Ⓜ Staroměstská

LUCERNA MUSIC BAR
This is part of the vast complex of the Lucerna Palace, a labyrinth of arcades and passageways that were the work of President Havel's builder-grandfather. Its good-sized ballroom can accommodate visiting groups as well as locals, and although some expats look down on it, it's the place to go for Czech retro.

➕ E5 ✉ Vodičkova 36, Nové město ☎ 2421 7108
Ⓜ Můstek

MALOSTRANSKÁ BESEDA
Something for everyone—ska, folk, reggae, blues, rock. You might even catch the Original Prague Syncopated Orchestra, with its immaculate re-creation of vintage swing. Before or after the music you can relax in the café-cum-gallery that also occupies the premises.

➕ D4 ✉ Malostranské náměstí 21, Malá Strana
☎ 53 90 24 Ⓜ Malostranská
🚋 Tram 22, 23 to Malostranské náměstí

PALÁC AKROPOLIS
In the shadow of the television tower (➤ 51), this is the city's main venue for world music and alternative acts. There's a dance club, too. The funky pub on the premises is popular with younger expats and locals.

➕ G5 ✉ Kubelíkova 3, Vinohrady ☎ 2271 2287
Ⓜ Jiřího z Poděbrad

RADOST FX
A serious dance scene prevails at one of the city's most well-known clubs.

➕ F6 ✉ Bělehradská 120, Vinohrady ☎ 2425 4776
Ⓜ I.P. Pavlova

ROCK CAFÉ
This downtown café and concert spot is the place to go if you like your rock music hard and very loud.

➕ E5 ✉ Národní 20, Nové město ☎ 2491 4414
Ⓜ Národní třída

ROXY
Unusual underground establishment that has DJs and live acts of every conceivable stripe.

➕ E4 ✉ Dlouhá 33, Staré město ☎ 2482 6390
Ⓜ Náměstí Republiky

Rock Czech-style
Before 1989, groups like the Plastic People of the Universe were seen as genuinely subversive of the existing order and were relentlessly hounded by State Security. Nowadays, the rock scene is a confused one, with a lot of fairly mindless imitation of Western trends but some innovation too, by groups like Šum Svistu (Latin influenced) and Shalom (obsessed by Judaism).

Jazz, Cabaret & Casinos

Prague jazz

Jazz has deep roots among the Czech people, as evidenced in the novels and short stories of the long-exiled writer Josef Škvorecký (for example, *The Bass Saxophone*). The Prague jazz scene is highly concentrated, with most venues clustered in the area between the Národní divadlo (National Theater) and Václavské náměstí (Wenceslas Square).

JAZZ

AGHARTA JAZZ CENTRUM
Cramped but enjoyable for local and international jazz, with cocktails and snacks. CD shop.
✚ F5 ✉ Krakovská 5, Nové město ☎ 2221 1275
Ⓜ Muzeum

JAZZ CLUB U STARÉ PANÍ
Some of the best local musicians play in this central jazz club.
✚ E4 ✉ Michalská 9, Staré město ☎ 2422 8090
Ⓜ Můstek

JAZZ CLUB ŽELEZNÁ
Another minuscule club for jazzers, this one is in ancient cellars in the heart of the Old Town. The music varies from swing to blues to Latin.
✚ E4 ✉ Železná 16, Staré město ☎ 2423 9697
Ⓜ Můstek

METROPOLITAN
Swing, ragtime, and blues.
✚ E5 ✉ Jungmannova 14, Nové město ☎ 2494 7777
Ⓜ Národní třída or Můstek

REDUTA
Bill Clinton blew his sax at this best-known of Prague jazz locales during his presidential visit to Prague in 1994. You can hear Dixieland, swing, and modern jazz.
✚ E5 ✉ Národní 20, Nové město ☎ 2491 2246
Ⓜ Národní třída

U MALÉHO GLENA
Little Glenn's is named after its genial owner, who provides recorded jazz in the candlelit upstairs bar and the real thing—alternating with pop and rock—in the tiny basement.
✚ D4 ✉ Karmelitská 23, Malá Strana ☎ 535 8115
🚋 Tram 12, 22, 23 to Malostranské náměstí

UNGELT JAZZ 'N' BLUES CLUB
More pub than club, this newish place concentrates on local talent.
✚ E4 ✉ Týn 2 (enter from Týnská ulička), Staré město ☎ 2489 5748 Ⓜ Můstek or Staroměstská

CASINOS & CABARETS

If you want to see a good old-fashioned floor show, with music, dancing, and spectacle, the larger hotels are the best bet. Reserve a place in advance.

CASINO HILTON ATRIUM
Roulette and other games, in spacious, modern surroundings.
✚ F3 ✉ Prague Hilton Atrium, Pobřežní 1, Karlín ☎ 2484 2005 Ⓜ Florenc

CASINO PALAIS SAVARIN
Roulette and other games.
✚ E4 ✉ Na příkopě 10, Nové město ☎ 2422 1636
Ⓜ Můstek or Náměstí Republiky

VARIETÉ PRAGA
Variety, brass bands, and gaming in a wonderful building in art-nouveau style.
✚ E5 ✉ Vodičkova 30, Nové město ☎ 2421 5945
Ⓜ Můstek

MULTIMEDIA THEATER & MIME

ČERNÉ DIVADLO JIŘÍHO SRNCE (JIŘÍ SRNEC BLACK THEATER)

Legends of magic Prague presented in multimedia format.

⊞ E4 ✉ Celetná 17, Staré město ☎ 5792 3397 🚇 Náměstí Republiky Also at ⊞ E5 ✉ Lucerna Ballroom, Štěpánská 61, Nové město 🚇 Můstek

ČESKÝ SOUBOR PÍSNÍ A TANCŮ (CZECH FOLKLORE ENSEMBLE)

Well-rehearsed rustic song and dance troupe with a long tradition.

⊞ B4 ✉ Hotel Pyramida, Bělohorská 24, Střešovice ☎ 3337 3475 🚋 Tram 8, 22, 23 to Malovanka

DIVADLO IMAGE (IMAGE THEATER)

Visitor-oriented theater with black light shows, featuring dance, mime, and music.

⊞ E4 ✉ Pařížská 4, Staré město ☎ 232 9191 🚇 Staroměstská

DIVADLO MIMŮ ALFRED VE DVOŘE (ALFRED IN THE COURTYARD MIME THEATER)

Ctibor Turba's mime troupe no longer performs here, but the venue hosts visiting performers.

⊞ F3 ✉ Františka Křížka 36, Holešovice 🚋 Tram 5, 12, 17 to Veletržní

KONGRESOVÉ CENTRUM (CONGRESS CENTER)

Big-budget Czech-language musicals and other events are staged in the city's largest auditorium, once the gathering place for Communist Party bigwigs.

⊞ F7 ✉ 5. května 1640/65, Vyšehrad ☎ 6117 4444 🚇 Vyšehrad

LATERNA MAGIKA

The Magic Lantern's synthesis of film, music, theater, and mime was first developed in the 1950s by Alfréd Radok, and continues to intrigue and delight audiences. Some of the most successful shows are reworkings of ancient myths.

⊞ D/E5 ✉ Nová scéna of the National Theater, Národní 4, Nové město ☎ 2491 4129 🚇 Národní třída

TA FANTASTIKA

Another spectacle based on the black light fusion of dance, mime, and music—a spin-off from the hugely successful Laterna Magika. The stage also hosts pop musicals starring local idols.

⊞ E4 ✉ Karlova 8, Staré město ☎ 2222 1366 🚇 Staroměstská

Keeping you posted

Since 1989 there has been a boom in performances of all kinds intended to appeal to foreign visitors. You don't have to speak Czech to enjoy mime and multimedia (known locally as black light theater), big on the Prague stage. Most such shows are for foreign visitors, who can also enjoy performances of Czech folk art at various locations. Posters and leaflets will keep you up to date about what's on, as will the English-language *Prague Post* weekly newspaper.

Movies

Prague has dozens of movie theaters, many around Wenceslas Square. Recent releases are often shown in the original version with Czech subtitles.

DRAMA & PUPPETRY

Czech puppetry

In a country where the art of manipulating marionettes is taught in universities, no one whose imagination has been stimulated by the array of delightful little figures on sale on stalls and in stores should miss one of Prague's puppet performances. The colorful characters are mostly drawn from the fairy tales that are such a feature of Czech popular literature. They include water sprites and witches, devils, soldiers, and highwaymen, villains and virgins.

DIVADLO ARCHA (ARCHA THEATER)
Archa hosts superb productions of avant-garde theater. Tickets for most shows are inexpensive and highly sought after.
✚ F4 ✉ Na poříčí 26, north Nové město ☎ 232 8800 Ⓜ Náměstí Republiky

DIVADLO JIŘÍHO GROSSMANNA (JIŘÍ GROSSMANN THEATER)
Some non-Czech performances are put on in this establishment.
✚ E5 ✉ Václavské náměstí 43, Nové město ☎ 2422 8814 Ⓜ Můstek

DIVADLO MINOR (MINOR THEATER)
This well-known children's puppetry and drama ensemble currently operates from the Comedy Theater, with occasional shows elsewhere.
✚ E5 ✉ Divadlo Komedie, Jungmannova 1, Nové město ☎ 2223 2530 Ⓜ Národní třída

DIVADLO NA ZÁBRADLÍ (THEATER ON THE BALUSTRADE)
Václav Havel shifted scenery here. Later, his plays helped build the theater's reputation.
✚ E4 ✉ Anenské náměstí 5, Staré město ☎ 2222 2026 Ⓜ Staroměstská

DIVADLO SPEJBLA A HURVÍNKA (SPEJBL AND HURVÍNEK THEATER)
Don't miss the antics of Prague's immortal puppet duo: Josef Skupa's troubled father and his perky son have been performing in their own theater since 1945.
✚ C3 ✉ Dejvická 38 ☎ 2431 6784 Ⓜ Dejvická

DIVADLO V CELETNÉ (CELETNÁ THEATER)
The most frequent venue for shows by Prague's two resident English-language ensembles, Black Box and Misery Loves Company. The Jiří Srnec Black Theater also performs here (► 79).
✚ E4 ✉ Celetná 17, Staré město ☎ 232 6843 Ⓜ Náměstí Republiky

GLOBE THEATER
In the summertime, Shakespeare is staged in Prague's own low-budget replica of The Bard's home stage. Some productions are performed in English.
✚ E/F2 ✉ Výstaviště (Exhibition Grounds), Holešovice ☎ 2010 3608 🚋 Tram 5, 12, 17 to Výstaviště

NÁRODNÍ DIVADLO (NATIONAL THEATER)
You can see classics of Czech theater here, as well as performances of opera and ballet.
✚ D/E5 ✉ Národní 2, Nové město ☎ 2491 3437 Ⓜ Národní třída

NÁRODNÍ DIVADLO MARIONET (NATIONAL MARIONETTE THEATER)
Adaptations of operas are among the attractions. There are matinees for youngsters.
✚ E4 ✉ Žatecká 1, Staré město ☎ 2481 9522 Ⓜ Staroměstská

SPORTS & OUTDOOR ACTIVITIES

SOCCER

SPARTA STADIUM
First-class soccer at the home of Sparta, one of the country's leading teams.
✚ E3 ✉ Milady Horákové 98 ☎ 2057 0323 🚊 Tram 26 to Sparta

ICE HOCKEY

PAEGAS ARENA
This big indoor venue is the base of H.C. Sparta Praha ice hockey team.
✚ F2 ✉ Výstaviště (Exhibition Grounds), Holešovice ☎ 872 7477 🚊 Tram 5, 12, 17 to Výstaviště

SKATING

SPORTS HALL
One of several indoor ice rinks in Prague. In winter there's also skating on ponds, lakes, and reservoirs on the outskirts of Prague.
✚ F2 ✉ Výstaviště (Exhibition Grounds), Holešovice ☎ 2010 3204 🚇 Nádraží Holešovice 🚊 Tram 5, 12, 17 to Výstaviště

SWIMMING

HOSTIVAŘ RESERVOIR
Prague's biggest reservoir; you can go windsurfing, boating, and swimming.
✚ Off map, 7.5 miles southeast of Prague 🚇 Háje, then walk or bus 165, 170, 212, 213

PLAVECKÝ STADION PODOLÍ (PODOLÍ POOLS)
Large complex of pools, sauna, and such.
✚ E8 ✉ Podolská 74, Podolí ☎ 4143 3952 🚊 Tram 3, 17 to Kublov

SLAPY DAM & LAKE
The Vltava upstream from Prague has been dammed to form a chain of lakes with beaches made of imported sand.
✚ Off map, 20 miles south of Prague 🚌 Bus from Na Knížecí bus station (Metro Anděl)

BIKING

PŮJČOVNA SERVIS SPORT
One of the few places in Prague to rent bikes.
✚ G5 ✉ Šumavská 33, Vinohrady ☎ 2425 6121 🚇 Náměstí Míru 🚊 Tram 16 to Šumavská

HORSE RACING

ZÁVODIŠTĚ CHUCHLE (CHUCHLE RACECOURSE)
Flat races and trotting.
✚ Off map, 6 miles south of Prague ☎ 5794 1042 🚇 Suburban train from Smíchov to Velká Chuchle 🚌 Bus 172

GOLF

GOLF CLUB MOTOL
A basic nine-hole course in the western suburbs.
✚ Off map, 4 miles west of downtown. Plzeňská 215, Motol ☎ 5721 5185 🚇 Anděl then tram 4, 7, or 9 to the Hotel Golf stop

KARLŠTEJN
One of a number of newish courses; this one has the benefit of Hrad Karlštejn (Karlštejn Castle ► 20) as a backdrop.
✚ Off map, 20 miles to the southwest ☎ 0311 684716

In-town biking
Bicycling is not particularly popular in this fume- and cobble-ridden city. On weekends urban bicyclists congregate in the city's extensive Stromovka Park, where there is a network of marked bicycle paths and some signposting indicating how bicyclists might reach other parts of Prague in relative safety.

LUXURY HOTELS

Prices

Expect to pay Kč5,000 or more for a double room in a luxury hotel.

Reserve ahead

Until recently, Prague suffered from an acute shortage of hotel accommodations, particularly in the middle price range, and was not an inexpensive place to stay. The situation has improved, but it is always wise to reserve well in advance, especially in summer and if you want to stay downtown.

ADRIA

A stunningly restored old establishment set amid the glitter and bustle of Wenceslas Square. With 88 rooms.

🞢 E5 ✉ Václavské náměstí 26 ☎ 2108 1111; fax 2108 1300 🚇 Můstek

DON GIOVANNI

A rather gaudy modern building neighboring the cemetery where Franz Kafka is buried, this 398-room hotel offers every service to business and leisure travelers at lower prices than many Prague luxury hotels.

🞢 J5 ✉ Vinohradská 157a, Vinohrady ☎ 6703 1111; fax 6703 6717 🚇 Želivského

HOFFMEISTER

In a refurbished historic building, this luxurious 39-room hotel prides itself on its personalized service. It is enviably sited on the road up to Prague Castle.

🞢 D3 ✉ Pod bruskou 7 ☎ 5101 7111; fax 5101 7120 🚇 Malostranská

HOLIDAY INN PRAGUE

A long-established 243-room hotel in the northern suburbs, in a Socialist-Realist skyscraper, with all the atmosphere of the Stalinist 1950s.

🞢 C2 ✉ Koulova 15, Dejvice ☎ 2439 3111; fax 2431 0616 🚇 Dejvická 🚊 Tram 20, 25 to Podbaba

INTERCONTINENTAL

This 364-room hotel was hypermodern and the epitome of pretension in Communist days, when it opened back in the 1970s. Near Josefov, it has every comfort, as well as spacious public rooms furnished with antiques.

🞢 E3 ✉ Náměstí Curieových 5 ☎ 2488 1111; fax 2481 1216 🚇 Staroměstská

JALTA

The air-conditioned 89-room Jalta is a fine example of 1950s architecture, and has an unbeatable position towards the top of Wenceslas Square.

🞢 F5 ✉ Václavské náměstí 45 ☎ 2422 9133; fax 2421 3866 🚇 Muzeum or Můstek

PALACE

A sumptuous art-nouveau exterior conceals the refurbished and eminently comfortable interior of this 124-room hotel.

🞢 E4 ✉ Panská 12 ☎ 2409 3111; fax 2422 1240 🚇 Můstek

PAŘÍŽ

Rampant early 1900s splendor, with 93 rooms, in Staré město.

🞢 E4 ✉ U Obecního domu 1 ☎ 2422 2151; fax 2219 5195 🚇 Náměstí Republiky

PRAGUE HILTON ATRIUM

Around the vast interior atrium of the city's largest hotel are 788 rooms, enough to house Bill Clinton's entourage during his presidential visit to Prague in 1994.

🞢 F3 ✉ Pobřežní 1 ☎ 2484 1111; fax 2484 2378 🚇 Florenc

PRAHA

The Praha perfectly expresses the way

Communist taste moved from the Stalinist certainties of the International Hotel in the 1950s (now the Holiday Inn ➤ 82) to the anonymous luxury of the 1970s. Until 1989, the 124-room Praha, in its hilltop location in the western suburb of Dejvice, was reserved for privileged and powerful Party people and their guests.

➕ B2 ✉ Sušická 20, Dejvice ☎ 2434 1111; fax 2431 1218 Ⓜ Dejvická 🚋 Tram 2, 20, 26 to Hadovka

RENAISSANCE

A comfortable, modern, 314-room hotel with all the facilities for business travelers. Tourists will appreciate its location a block from the Municipal House and the stores along Na příkopě. Operated by the Marriott organization.

➕ F4 ✉ V Celnici 7, Nové město ☎ 2182 1111; fax 2182 2200 Ⓜ Náměstí Republiky

SAVOY

Top-of-the-market luxury near Prague Castle. This 61-room hotel has been completely modernized.

➕ C4 ✉ Keplerova 6 ☎ 2430 2430; fax 2430 2128 🚋 Tram 22, 23 to Pohořelec

UNGELT

Nine-room apartment hotel in ancient premises that once formed part of the city's customs house, in Staré město.

➕ E4 ✉ Malá Štupartská 1 ☎ 2482 8686; fax 2482 8181 Ⓜ Náměstí Republiky

U PÁVA

"The Peacock" preens itself on its perfect location by the Vojan Gardens in lower Malá Strana, a few short steps from Charles Bridge. It has 11 rooms.

➕ D4 ✉ U lužického semináře 32 ☎ 5732 0743; fax 53 33 79 Ⓜ Malostranská

U RAKA

Idyllically located among the stuccoed houses of Nový Svět. Extremely comfortable, rather exclusive.

➕ C4 ✉ Černínská 10 ☎ 2051 1100; fax 2051 0511 🚋 Tram 22, 23 to Brusnice

U TŘÍ PŠTROSŮ

"The Three Ostriches," in an exquisite gabled Renaissance building, was once the center of a flourishing feather trade, later a coffeehouse. From some of the 18 rooms you can almost exchange a handshake with people passing by on Charles Bridge.

➕ D4 ✉ Dražického náměstí 12 ☎ 5753 2410; fax 5753 3217 🚋 Tram 12, 22, 23 to Malostranské náměstí

VILLA VOYTA

The staff at this 20-room hotel in the southern suburbs cater to their mostly business clientele with great care, both in the original Secession villa and in the modern addition across the street.

➕ Off map, south of downtown ✉ K novému dvoru 124/54, Lhotka ☎ 6171 1307; fax 472 2918 Ⓜ Kačerov, then bus 106, 150, 170, 196, 203 to Sulická

Accommodations advice

Any number of agencies at the airport, the main railroad station (Hlavní nádraží), and Holešovice railroad station stand ready to help you with advice on accommodations.

Two helpful agencies elsewhere are Accommodation Service (✉ Haštalská 7, Staré město ☎ 231 0202), which offers apartments in the Old Town and further afield, and Stop City (✉ Vinohradská 24, Vinohrady ☎ 2252 1252), which rents a range of accommodations, mostly in the Vinohrady area.

A small apartment for two people in a good part of the city costs around Kč1,500–2,500 per night. Prague Information Service (Pražská informační služba— PIS ☎ 2171 4130), the official city information agency, will also find lodgings. It has offices at the main railroad station, Old Town Square and Na příkopě (➤ 19).

MID-RANGE HOTELS

Prices

Expect to pay Kč2,500–5,000 for a double room in a mid-range hotel.

Breathe freely

Choosing a place to stay requires care. A central location may turn out to be noisy with traffic as the rush hour gets under way shortly after 5AM. Somewhere in the suburbs may seem a long way from the action, but if the hotel is near a Metro station, this is unlikely to be a problem, and your night's rest may be more relaxed because you are breathing air that is fresher (albeit marginally so).

AMETYST

A fresh and inviting 84-room, family-owned hotel, the equal in luxury to most of the big names and only 10 minutes' walk from Wenceslas Square.

➕ F6 ✉ Jana Masaryka 11, Vinohrady ☎ 2425 4185; fax 2425 1315 🚇 Náměstí Míru

ATLANTIK

A pleasant alternative to the Harmony (➤ below) if you want to stay on this busy shopping street close to downtown. Atlantik has 60 rooms.

➕ F4 ✉ Na poříčí 9 ☎ 2481 1084; fax 2481 2378 🚇 Náměstí Republiky

BETLEM CLUB

A small 22-room hotel offering accommodations in the same square as Jan Hus's historic Bethlehem Chapel.

➕ E4 ✉ Betlémské náměstí 9 ☎ 2222 1574; fax 2222 0580 🚇 Národní třída

BÍLÁ LABUŤ

A Best Western hotel, with 55 rooms, a short walk from Náměstí Republiky.

➕ F4 ✉ Biskupská 9 ☎ 2481 1382; fax 232 2905 🚇 Náměstí Republiky

CENTRAL

Somewhat run-down but quite adequate. Behind the Municipal House, with 68 rooms.

➕ E4 ✉ Rybná 8 ☎ 2481 2041 or 2481 2734; fax 232 8404 🚇 Náměstí Republiky

CITY HOTEL MORAN

Austrian-style elegance and comfort in a historic building close to Charles Square and the river. City Hotel Moran is a Best Western hotel.

➕ E6 ✉ Na Moráni 15 ☎ 2491 5208 🚇 Karlovo náměstí

CLOISTER INN

Basic accommodations combined with comparatively good service are the attractions at this 48-room hotel between the National Theater and the Bethlehem Chapel.

➕ E4 ✉ Konviktská 14, Staré město ☎ 2421 1020; fax 2421 0800 🚇 Národní třída

EVROPA

Nothing could be closer to Prague's heart than this art-nouveau jewel on Wenceslas Square. But most of the 92 rooms fail to live up to the promise of the resplendent facade.

➕ E5 ✉ Václavské náměstí 25 ☎ 2422 8117; fax 2422 4544 🚇 Můstek

HARMONY

In a 1930s building just east of the Municipal House, Harmony has 60 pleasant rooms. It is well suited for shoppers, on the busy Na poříčí.

➕ F4 ✉ Na poříčí 31 ☎ 232 0016; fax 231 0009 🚇 Náměstí Republiky

HOTEL 16 U SV. KATEŘINY

Well-priced family hotel, with 14 rooms. Just around the corner from the Dvořák Museum and 10 minutes' walk from Wenceslas Square.

➕ E5 ✉ Kateřinská 16 ☎ 2492 0636; fax 2492 0626 🚇 I.P. Pavlova

KAMPA

In a delightful corner of the Lesser Town close to the Devil's Brook, this old 84-bedroom building is popular with tour groups.

🚻 D4/5 ✉ Všehrdova 16 ☎ 5732 0404; fax 5732 0262 🚋 Tram 12, 22, 23 to Hellichova

NOVOMĚSTSKÝ HOTEL

A small hotel on a quiet street by the New Town Hall, with a high standard considering the relatively low room rates.

🚻 E5 ✉ Řeznická 4, Nové město ☎ 2223 1498 🚇 Karlovo náměstí

OBORA

Well-appointed 21-room hotel in the royal hunting park and near Hvězda Castle, close to the airport.

🚻 Off map, west of downtown ✉ Libocká 271/1 ☎ 3535 7779; fax 3536 6093 🚇 Hradčanská, then tram 1, 18 to Petřiny

OLŠANKA

This large complex has two main attractions: inexpensive, simple rooms and an array of fringe benefits like a tennis court, large pool, weight room and sauna.

🚻 H5 ✉ Táboritská 23, Žižkov ☎ 6709 2202 🚋 Tram 5, 9, 26 to Olšanské náměstí

OPERA

Resembling a pink, frosted wedding cake, the Opera anchors a clutch of moderately-priced hotels in the vicinity of Na poříčí street in the north of the New Town. Completely renovated, it offers guests well-equipped, if functional rooms.

🚻 F3 ✉ Těšnov 13, Nové město ☎ 231 5609 🚇 Florenc

PÁV

A family-run, eight-room pension in a side street in Nové město where you'll also find Prague's most popular beer hall.

🚻 E5 ✉ Křemencova 13 ☎ 2491 3286; fax 2491 0574 🚇 Národní třída

PENSION DIENTZENHOFER

In a secluded side street in Malá Strana, this seven-room pension is the former home of the Dientzenhofers, greatest of Prague's baroque architects.

🚻 D4 ✉ Nosticova 2 ☎ 53 16 72; fax 5732 0888 🚋 Tram 12, 22, 23 to Hellichova

SAX

You can't get closer to Prague Castle than this 22-room hotel just off Nerudova Street.

🚻 C4 ✉ Janský vršek 3 ☎ 5753 1268; fax 5753 4101 🚋 Tram 12, 22, 23 to Malostranské náměsti then an uphill walk

U KRÁLE JIŘÍHO

Just off the Royal Way, with 11 comfortable rooms and the dubious bonus of a pub on the first floor.

🚻 E4 ✉ Liliová 10 ☎ 2222 0925; fax 2222 1707 🚇 Staroměstská

Special offers

The number of moderately priced hotels has increased rapidly, but these properties are probably still outnumbered by expensive hotels. However, it's always worth checking to see if the latter are offering any special deals, particularly for weekend stays.

Botels

An alternative to conventional hotels are the "botels" moored at various points along the banks of the Vltava. However, they are rather cramped and so are less romantic than they might sound. One such, close to the Palacký Bridge (Palackého most) on the Smíchov quayside, is the Admirál (☎ 5732 1302).

BUDGET ACCOMMODATIONS

Prices

Expect to pay Kč1,000–2,500 for a double room in budget accommodations.

Home away from home

An economical solution to the problem of accommodations is to stay in a private house or, more likely, to rent an apartment. Most agencies have such places on their books, and going through one of them is better than allowing yourself to be solicited on arrival. Private rooms can also be booked from abroad. Check that you won't have to change buses and trams three times to get into town from your accommodations.

ANNA

A reliable 23-room hotel in the pleasant inner suburb of Vinohrady, less than 15 minutes' stroll from Wenceslas Square.

✚ G5 ✉ Budečská 17, Vinohrady ☎ 2251 3111; fax 2251 5158 🚇 Náměstí Míru

BERN

Reasonable comfort and facilities, rock-bottom prices at this simple hotel a brief bus ride east of downtown.

✚ G4 ✉ Koněvova 28, Žižkov ☎ 697 4420 🚇 Florenc, then bus 133, 207 to Tachovské

BÍLÝ LEV

A good-value, 27-room establishment in the eastern suburb of Žižkov.

✚ G4 ✉ Cimburkova 20 ☎ 2278 0430; fax 2278 2190 🚊 Trams 5, 9, 26 to Husinecká

CITY PENSION

Exceptionally pleasant 19-room pension, one Metro stop from Wenceslas Square.

✚ F6 ✉ Belgická 10 ☎ 2252 1606; fax 2252 2386 🚇 Náměstí Míru

COUBERTIN

A modern 31-room hotel named after the founder of the modern Olympics, and located among the Strahov sports facilities.

✚ B5 ✉ Atletická 4, Strahov ☎ 3335 3109; fax 2051 3208 🚇 Dejvická, then bus 149, 217 to Stadion Strahov

GOLF

This 163-room motel is handily located on the main road that heads into the city from the west.

✚ Off map, west of downtown. ✉ Plzeňská 215a, Motol ☎ 5721 5185; fax 5721 5213 🚇 Anděl, then tram 7, 9, 10, 58 to Hotel Golf

HOSTEL BOATHOUSE

This welcoming hostel occupies a real boathouse on the river bank, a half-hour journey south of downtown by tram. Cash only.

✚ Off map, south of downtown ✉ Lodnická 1, Braník ☎ 402 1076 🚊 Trams 3, 17, 54 to Černý kůň

KAFKA

A 50-room hotel with bargain rates on the wrong side of the tracks in the seedy inner suburb of Žižkov, but only 10 minutes' walk from the main railroad station and a short tram ride to Wenceslas Square.

✚ G4 ✉ Cimburkova 24 ☎ 2278 1333; fax 5732 7862 🚊 tram 5, 9, 26 to Husinecká

LOUDA

Pleasant eight-room pension on a residential road off the main highway to northern Bohemia and eastern Germany.

✚ H1 ✉ Kubišova 10 ☎ 688 1491; fax 688 1488 🚇 Nádraží Holešovice, then Tram 5, 14, 17 to Hercovka

TŘÍSKA

A friendly place well sited in the pleasant Vinohrady neighborhood. Each of the funkily-furnished rooms has a refrigerator. Cash only.

✚ G5 ✉ Vinohradská 105, Vinohrady ☎ 627 0662 🚇 Jiřího z Poděbrad

PRAGUE
travel facts

ARRIVING & DEPARTING

Before you go

- Visas are not required for citizens of the United States for a stay of up to 30 days. However, a change in the regulations means Canadian visitors must now obtain a visa before traveling.

When to go

- The best times to visit are in spring, when the fruit trees of Petřín Hill are in blossom, and in early summer.
- Winter weather can be depressingly gray and cold, with high levels of air pollution.
- High summer can become oppressively hot and humid, with considerable rainfall.
- Most tourists visit between May and September. Christmas and New Year can also be busy.

Arriving by air

- There are direct flights to Ruzyně Airport from New York, Toronto, and Montreal.
- Prague is served by ČSA, the national airline, as well as by other major carriers.
- The best downtown link is by airport bus, either to Dejvická Metro station or to Náměstí Republiky on the eastern edge of the Old Town. City bus 119 also goes to Dejvická station. For taxis, ► 91.
- The ČSA main office is at ✉ V celnici 5, Nové město ☎ 2010 4111

Arriving by train

- Express trains connect Prague to all neighboring countries, as well as to Paris, from where passengers can take the Eurostar Channel Tunnel rail link to London.
- Most trains terminate at Hlavní nádraží (Main Station ✚ F4),

though some stop (or terminate) at Holešovice in the northern suburbs or at Smíchov in the southern suburbs, both of which have good Metro connections.
- Czech Railways (ČD) has information offices in Main Station at the north end of level 3 (domestic) and the south end of the lower hall (international) ☎ 2422 4200

Arriving by car

- Good main roads link Prague to all neighboring countries, and the highway to Plzeň (Pilsen) and the border with Bavaria is almost complete. Prague is less than 700 miles from Calais, with its ferry services to Dover as well as the Channel Tunnel Shuttle. To drive on certain major Czech highways you need a toll sticker, which can be bought at the border or at post offices (Kč100 for 10 days, Kč200 for a month, or Kč800 for a year).
- Check that your insurance policy covers you to drive in the Czech Republic. You may need to purchase temporary insurance at the border.
- The drink-drive limit is zero alcohol.

Arriving by bus

- Express buses link Prague with international destinations, including London.
- The main coach terminal is at Florenc, on the eastern edge of downtown, where there is a Metro station.
- Departure tickets can be obtained at the coach terminal at Florenc, but it is easier to buy them through a travel agency.

Arriving by boat

- Occasional passenger boats ply the Vltava and Elbe to Dresden and on to Hamburg.

Customs regulations

- The duty-free allowance comprises 200 cigarettes or 100 cigars or 250g tobacco; 2 liters of wine; 1 liter of liquor; and personal items totalling Kč6,000 in value.
- There is no limit on the import or export of foreign currencies.
- In principle, there are strict limits on the export of goods purchased in the Czech Republic, but normal tourist souvenirs are unlikely to pose any problem. However, antiques and "rare cultural objects" require an official certificate from a recognized museum or art gallery (which the dealer may already have obtained).
- The import of wildlife souvenirs sourced from rare or endangered species may be illegal or require a special permit. Before purchase you should check your home country's customs regulations.

ESSENTIAL FACTS

Travel insurance

- Check your insurance policies to make sure you will be covered for accident, illness, loss, and other eventualities.

Opening hours

- Banks: Mon–Fri 8–5.
- Stores: Many downtown stores stay open until late weekdays and are also open weekends. In the suburbs and elsewhere, stores are open Mon–Fri 9–6; Sat 9–1.
- Museums and galleries: Tue–Sun 9/10–5. Most close Mon, except the National Museum and Prague Castle (open daily); the Jewish Museum is open Sun–Fri. Some museums also close for lunch.

National holidays

- January 1, Easter Monday, May 1 (Labor Day), May 8 (Liberation Day), July 5 (SS Cyril and Methodius), July 6 (Jan Hus's Day), September 28 (St. Wenceslas's Day), October 28 (Independence Day), November 17 (Day of Students), December 24–26.

Money matters

- The Czech crown (*koruna česká* or Kč) is divided into 100 virtually worthless hellers (*halér*).
- There are coins for 10, 20, and 50 hellers, and for 1, 2, 5, 10, 20, and 50 crowns, and notes in denominations of 50, 100, 200, 500, 1,000, 2,000, and 5,000 crowns.
- There are plenty of bureaux de change, but banks and ATMs often give better exchange rates.
- Credit cards are in increasing use, particularly in tourist spots.

Etiquette

- Czech manners tend to be formal. Titles such as Doctor and Professor must not be ignored, and hands should be shaken when offered.
- Dress is less formal than it used to be. Neat casual wear is acceptable in most restaurants and tourist theaters, while in other theaters and at the opera men should wear suits and women dress smartly.
- Diners share tables in crowded restaurants, and exchange greetings such as "*dobrý den*" ("good day"), "*dobrou chuť*" ("enjoy your meal"), and "*na shledanou*" ("goodbye").
- If you are invited to a Czech home, take flowers or a gift and remove your shoes at the door.

Women travelers

- Women travelers need take no more than the usual precautions.
- At night, unaccompanied females

lingering in parts of Wenceslas Square may be taken for prostitutes.

Places of worship

- Roman Catholic: sv. Tomáše (St. Thomas's Church)
  - ✉ Josefská 8, Malá Strana 🚇 Malostranská
  - 🕐 English mass Sat 6PM; Sun 11AM
- Anglican: sv. Klimenta (St. Clement's Church)
  - ✉ Klimentská, Nové město 🚇 Náměstí Republiky
  - 🕐 English-language service Sun 11AM
- Jewish: Staronová synagóga (Old/New Synagogue ➤ 39)
  - ✉ Pařížská and Červená 🚇 Staroměstská
  - 🕐 Services Mon–Thu 8AM; Fri sundown; Sat 9AM

Student travelers

- Few discounts are available for students, but keeping out of the most popular tourist spots makes Prague an affordable city to get by in.
- All aspects of youth travel are dealt with by the GTS agency
  - ✉ Ve Smečkách 27, Nové město ☎ 9622 4300
  - 🚇 Muzeum

Time differences

- Central European Time applies (six hours ahead of US Standard Time), changed for daylight saving between March and October.

Rest rooms

- "WC," "OO," "*muži/páni*" (Men), and "*ženy/dámy*" (Women) are useful signs to remember.
- Public facilities are rare; look in restaurants, cafés, etc.
- Tip the attendant (usually an old woman) with some smaller coins—these are her wages.

Electricity

- 230 volts, 50 cycles AC, fed through standard Continental two-pin plugs.

PUBLIC TRANSPORTATION

- Prague's comprehensive transportation system is based on the immaculate underground Metro and the less pristine but equally reliable trams and buses.
- Day services run from 5AM to midnight, when infrequent night buses and trams take over.
- Inexpensive tickets obtained at stations, kiosks, and some hotels serve all three modes and must be validated by inserting into the clipping machine as you enter a station or board a vehicle. Normal tickets allow unlimited transfers among modes; non-transferable tickets are useful for brief trips.
- Public transportation maps are available from the Prague Information Service (➤ 19) and from the information centers at Metro stations Muzeum, Můstek, Anděl, Černý Most, and Nádraží Holešovice. They show all Metro and tram lines, as well as naming the tram stops and Metro stations.
- Expect crowding during the rush hours (generally 7AM–10AM, 3PM–6PM). The young and fit should give up their seats to passengers who need them more.

Metro

- This showpiece system, with its fast and frequent trains and clean stations, consists of three lines: A (color-coded green), B (yellow), and C (red). They converge from the suburbs onto downtown where there are several interchange stations.
- To get on the right train, check the line (A, B, or C) and note the name of the terminus station at the end of the line in the direction you wish to travel; this station appears on the overhead direction signs.

- Outlying stations are relatively far apart and are intended more to feed commuters to connecting trams and buses than to take tourists to their favorite spots.
- Particularly useful stations are Můstek (for Wenceslas Square and Old Town Square), Staroměstská (for Old Town Square), and Malostranská (for Malá Strana and for trams 22 and 23). Hradčanská station is 15 minutes' walk from Prague Castle.

Tram

- The tramway system operates in close conjunction with the Metro and can spare your legs on many of your likely itineraries.
- The name of every tram stop appears on the stop sign and on the route map.
- Tram routes are numbered, and the tram has a destination board. Timetables are pasted on the stop and are almost always adhered to.
- There is a skeleton service of night trams, with its own system of numbers and schedules.
- A particularly useful and scenic line is the No. 22/23, which runs from downtown (at Národní třída) right through Malá Strana, past Malostranská Metro station, then climbs to the back entrance of Prague Castle (Pražský hrad stop) or on to Strahov Monastery.

Bus

- Kept out of the downtown to minimize pollution, buses serve all the suburban areas that the trams do not reach.

Discounts

- Special passes are valid for periods of one day upwards but are useful only if you intend to make lots of trips.

Taxi

- Prague taxi drivers have earned a reputation for overcharging and being disagreeable.
- Agree on the approximate fare beforehand. Ask for a receipt to reduce excessive demands.
- You may receive a more reliable service if you phone for a taxi or flag down a moving taxi rather than going to a taxi rank in a tourist area, where drivers have the worst reputation.
- For taxis, telephone AAA Radiotaxi ☎ 14014 or Profitaxi ☎ 1035
- Upscale hotels have their own taxi service, reliable but expensive.

MEDIA & COMMUNICATIONS

Telephones

- Ongoing modernization of the Czech phone system means improved service. A continuing frustration is that numbers may change with little notice. If in doubt, call directory inquiries ☎ 1180.
- Most public phones now take phone cards, on sale in kiosks and post offices.
- Telephoning from your hotel may cost four times the standard rate.
- To call the Czech Republic from the United States, dial 011 420. The code for Prague is 2 (02 within the country). To call the US from Prague, dial 00 1, followed by the relevant city code and number.

Mail

- Postage stamps can be bought at post offices, kiosks, and hotels.
- The main post office, with fax and poste restante services, is at
✚ F4 ✉ Jindřišská 14, Nové město ☎ 2113 1445 Ⓜ Můstek

Newspapers and magazines

- Foreign-language newspapers are on sale at downtown news-stands and at some hotels.
- The leading English-language publication is the weekly *Prague Post*, with useful events listings.
- The English-language *Prague Business Journal* is much as its title suggests.
- The German-language weekly *Prager Zeitung* is for the Czech Republic's minuscule German population.

Radio and television

- Local TV consists of four channels—ČT1 and ČT2 (state-owned), and Nova and Prima (private). None is likely to interest those who don't speak Czech. Most hotels have multiple satellite channels.
- The BBC World Service can be picked up on 101.1 FM.
- Most local stations play commercial pop or rock's "golden oldies." Country Radio (89.5 FM) plays country music; Radio 1 (91.9 FM) plays avant-garde rock; and Classic FM (98.7 FM) plays classical music.

EMERGENCIES

Sensible precautions

- Despite some horror stories, Prague is still safer than most comparable Western cities.
- The main hazard is pickpockets in the tourist areas—Wenceslas Square, Charles Bridge, and Old Town Square. Hold onto your handbag and don't carry your wallet or passport in your back pocket.
- A common scam is for someone to accost you with an innocent-seeming inquiry about money or the location of the nearest bank.

His "policeman" accomplice will then appear and relieve you of your passport if you are unwise enough to produce it.

Lost property

- The lost property office is at ✉ Karoliny Světlé 5, Staré město ☎ 2423 5085

Medical treatment

- Emergency medical treatment is done under contract, so check your insurance policies in advance of your trip.
- Foreigners' Polyclinic ✉ Roentgenova 2, Motol (off map) ☎ 5727 2146; 5727 1111 (nights and weekends) 🚍 Bus 167 from Anděl Metro to the last stop Bring your passport to this former Communist Party clinic, which is part of the Nemocnice Na Homolce, the huge hospital complex just off the main highway to Pilsen in the western suburb of Motol. It is the best place to go for serious treatment.
- Fakultní poliklinika (✚ E5 ✉ Karlovo náměstí 32, Nové město ☎ 2490 4111 🕐 Mon–Fri 7–3:30 🚇 Karlovo náměstí) is a downtown alternative to the above for less serious ailments.
- Drugs prescribed locally must be paid for.
- Remember to bring supplies of any regular medication you take with you.
- 24-hour pharmacies are at ✉ Palackého 5, Nové město and ✉ Belgická 37, Vinohrady

Emergency phone numbers

- Ambulance ☎ 155
- Police ☎ 158
- Fire brigade ☎ 150

Embassy

- USA ✚ D4 ✉ Tržiště 15, Malá Strana ☎ 5753 0663 🚇 Malostranská, then Tram 12, 22 to Malostranské náměstí

LANGUAGE

- Czech is a Slavic language, so anyone who knows other Slavic languages, such as Russian or Polish, should have little difficulty in muddling through.
- It will be rewarding to master a few words and phrases, if only to be able to ask if anyone speaks your language and to recognize some signs.
- Czech is pronounced as it is written (unlike English).

Vowels

a	as in mammoth	á	as in father
e	as in yes	é	as in air
i,y	as in city	í,ý	as in meet
o	as in top	ó	as in more
u	as in book	ú,ů	as in boom

Consonants

c	as in its	č	as in china
ch	as in Scottish loch		
j	as in yes	ň	as in onion
r	rolled or trilled r	ř	combination of r and z (as in Dvořák)
š	as in shine		
z	as in zero	ž	as in pleasure

Basic words and phrases

yes ano
no ne
please prosím
thank you děkuji
do you speak English/German?
  mluvíte anglicky /německy?
I don't understand nerozumím
I don't speak Czech nemluvím česky
hello (informal) ahoj
good morning/good day dobrý den
good evening dobrý večer
goodbye na shledanou
sorry promiňte
where? kde?
how much? kolik?
when? kdy?
what? co?

Numbers

1	jeden/jedna/jedno	15	patnáct
2	dva/dvě	16	šestnáct
3	tři	17	sedmnáct
4	čtyři	18	osmnáct
5	pět	19	devatenáct
6	šest	20	dvacet
7	sedm	30	třicet
8	osm	40	čtyřicet
9	devět	50	padesát
10	deset	60	šedesát
11	jedenáct	70	sedmdesát
12	dvanáct	80	osmdesát
13	třináct	90	devadesát
14	čtrnáct	100	sto
		1,000	tisíc

Days of the week

Monday pondělí   Friday pátek
Tuesday úterý   Saturday sobota
Wednesday středa Sunday neděle
Thursday čvrtek

Months of the year

January leden   July červenec
February únor   August srpen
March březen   September září
April duben   October říjen
May květen   November listopad
June červen   December prosinec

Useful words

beer pivo
big velký/á/é
bus or tram stop zastávka
café kavárna
castle hrad
closed zavřeno
Danger! pozor!
entrance vchod/vstup
exit východ/výstup
forbidden zákaz
market trh
open otevřeno
pharmacy lékárna
pull (sign on door) sem
push (sign on door) tam
small malý/á/é
station nádraží
water voda

INDEX

Citypack
Prague

AUTHOR *Michael Ivory*
ORIGINAL DESIGN *Design FX*
COVER DESIGN *Fabrizio La Rocca,*
Tigist Getachew

COVER PICTURES *AA Photo Library*
THIRD EDITION REVISED BY
Ky Krauthamer

Copyright   © Automobile Association Developments Limited 1996, 1999, 2001
Maps copyright   © Automobile Association Developments Limited 1996, 1999, 2001
Fold-out map: © RV Reise- und Verkehrsverlag Munich · Stuttgart
                 © Cartography: GeoData

Published in the United Kingdom by AA Publishing

ISBN 0–676–90157–3
Third Edition

Acknowledgments

The Automobile Association wishes to thank the following photographers, associations, and libraries for their assistance in the preparation of this book: AKG, LONDON, 27; M. IVORY 25a, 25b; NATIONAL GALLERY IN PRAGUE 47; REX FEATURES LTD 12. All remaining pictures are held in the Association's own library (AA PHOTO LIBRARY), with contributions from C. Sawyer 1, 2, 5b, 13a, 13b, 18, 19, 20, 26b, 28a, 29, 30a, 32b, 36b, 37, 38b, 48a, 49b, 50, 52, 54, 55, 56, 58, 61b, 87b; A. SOUTER 5a, 7, 23b, 24, 33, 34, 36a, 41a, 42a, 46a, 46b, 87a; J. WYAND 6, 16, 17, 21a, 21b, 23a, 26a, 27, 28b, 30b, 31, 32a, 35a, 35b, 38a, 39, 40, 41b, 42b, 43, 44a, 44b, 45, 48b, 49a, 51, 57, 61a.

Important tip

Time inevitably brings changes, so always confirm prices, travel facts, and other perishable information when it matters. Although Fodor's cannot accept responsibility for errors, you can use this guide in the confidence that we have taken every care to ensure its accuracy.

Special sales

Fodor's Travel Publications are available at special discounts for bulk purchases (100 copies or more) for sales promotions or premiums. Special editions, including personalized covers, excerpts of existing guides, and corporate imprints, can be created in large quantities for special needs. For more information contact your local bookseller or write to Special Marketing, Fodor's Travel Publications, 280 Park Avenue, New York, NY 10017. Inquiries from Canada should be directed to your local Canadian bookseller or sent to Random House of Canada, Ltd., Marketing Department, 2775 Matheson Blvd. East, Mississauga, Ontario L4W 4P7.

Color separation by Daylight Colour Art Pte Ltd, Singapore
Manufactured by Dai Nippon Printing Co. (Hong Kong) Ltd.
10 9 8 7 6 5 4 3 2 1

Titles in the Citypack series